PRAISE FOR
ELAINE'S CIRCLE

"*Elaine's Circle* offers a gripping and moving account of how compassion can transform people in the most difficult of times. This is a book with lessons about empathy and helping children through tough times that every teacher and parent can benefit from."

—**Daniel Goleman,** author of *Emotional Intelligence*

"There are books that you read that stay with you all your life— *Elaine's Circle* will be one of them. Bob Katz has written an incredibly compelling and uplifting story about a magnificent teacher, her students, and a community who band together to help a dying child, and through that struggle learn the most important lessons of their lives. It's a book you have to read."

—**Lynne Cox,** author of *Swimming to Antarctica*

"This book is a gift. It's a reminder of the profound lessons that can happen daily in the classroom of a gifted teacher. *Elaine's Circle* is also a lesson about what children are capable of understanding when treated with honesty and respect."

—**Marc Brown,** author and executive producer of *Arthur,* the best-selling children's book and television series

"There is an enormous library of books on education—the theory, the practice. But Bob Katz here gives us a book that gets to the heart and soul of teaching, of learning, by telling an unforgettable story of one teacher, one class, one year, one fourth-grade child. Impending tragedy becomes an occasion for what should be the goal of all education—young people working together to have life triumph over death."

—**Howard Zinn,** author of *A People's History of the United States*

"Katz's book is about handling illness and death, and about teaching; Seamus's spunk, his teacher's perseverance, and his parents' dedication are quite moving."

—*Publishers Weekly*

"*Elaine's Circle* is a book about life. Whenever a book leads me to laughter and tears, I know it speaks the truth about life and has touched my heart. If you want a true education, read what a teacher and her pupils learned from the greatest of teachers, a child's death."

—**Dr. Bernie Siegel,** author of *Love, Medicine and Miracles, Help Me To Heal, 365 Prescriptions For The Soul,* and *Smudge Bunny*

"*Elaine's Circle* is a tragic, moving, and inspiring story that reminds us of two important things: children are less afraid of terminal illness than we think, and great teachers like Elaine Moore can turn even a child's impending death into a celebration of life."

—**Sam Swope,** author of *I Am a Pencil: A Teacher, His Kids, and Their World of Stories*

ABOUT THE AUTHOR

BOB KATZ is coauthor, with Bob Chase, of *The New Public School Parent*, hailed by best-selling author Mel Levine as "probably the best 'survival guide' for mothers and fathers who have kids in school" and author of the novel *Hot Air*. His writing has appeared in the *New York Times*, *Newsweek*, *Parents*, *USA Today*, *Mother Jones*, the *Chicago Tribune*, the *Nation*, the *Boston Globe*, *Parenting*, the *Christian Science Monitor*, *Newsday*, and many other publications. In addition, he has appeared on National Public Radio, CNN's *Talk Back Live*, ABC's *Good Morning America*, and many other TV and radio programs. He lives in Massachusetts.

ELAINE'S CIRCLE

ALSO BY BOB KATZ

The New Public School Parent
(with Bob Chase)

Hot Air

ELAINE'S CIRCLE

A TEACHER, A STUDENT, A CLASSROOM
AND ONE UNFORGETTABLE YEAR

BOB KATZ

MARLOWE & COMPANY
NEW YORK

ELAINE'S CIRCLE:
A Teacher, a Student, a Classroom and One Unforgettable Year

Copyright © 2005 by Bob Katz

Published by
Marlowe & Company
An Imprint of Avalon Publishing Group Incorporated
245 West 17th Street • 11th Floor
New York, NY 10011-5300

AVALON
publishing group incorporated

Library of Congress Cataloging-in-Publication Data
Katz, Robert A.
Elaine's circle : a teacher, a student, a classroom and one
unforgettable year / Bob Katz.
p. cm.
ISBN 1-56924-384-0 (pbk.)
1. Moore, Elaine, 1942– 2. Elementary school teachers—Alaska—Biography.
3. Teacher-student relationships—Alaska. 4. Public schools—Alaska. I. Title.
LA2317.M67 2005
372.11'0092—dc22
2005006944

9 8 7 6 5 4 3 2

Book design by Maria E. Torres

Printed in the United States of America

To my mother and father,
who taught me well.

CONTENTS

INTRODUCTION

This book began when I was starting work on another book. That project was tentatively titled "Class Acts" and was to consist of inspiring stories about teachers. It was to be a collection of real-life accounts, perhaps twenty to thirty altogether, highlighting the underpublicized yet compelling dramas that routinely take place in our nation's schools.

It was a good idea for a book (and remains one) in no small part because I was confident that vigorous research would uncover many such stories. My certainty was based on the experience I had had while researching a previous book, *The New Public School Parent*. In writing that book, I had immersed myself for many months in the world of public schools and had been struck by the abundance of vivid, moving stories there.

It seems to me that if you go into a school, almost any school, and spend a moderate amount of time talking with parents, administrators, teachers, and staff, it's almost guaranteed that eventually you will learn about some uplifting act of dedication, determination, sacrifice, or plain old magic. I am fully aware that the trendsetters of our culture are fixated on the notion that the valuable stories, the ones that really make people lean forward and plunk down dollars, are more likely to be found at crime scenes and battle zones. To my mind, schools are the great, untapped resource for stories of true heroism and passion.

To help the research for "Class Acts," I enlisted the assistance of several influential education groups known for their extensive network of contacts. I asked these groups to circulate, via newsletters and e-mail, a brief description of what I was looking for. My inquiry read:

> I am writing a book of uplifting (and true) stories about teachers and would like your help in identifying great stories to include. My main concern is that the story involve a specific event or a specific relationship between a teacher and a student or class.

I received a flood of interesting leads and suggestions. My method was to follow up with a phone call to make a quick assessment of the story's suitability to my purposes. Did it contain the human qualities I was seeking? Was there some underlying drama? Did it touch on deeper issues related to teaching and learning?

I was keenly aware that there was no precise definition of what I was looking for. I could only rely on the sort of navigational self-confidence that is often the best tool available to an eager seeker in an imprecise territory: I'd know it when I saw it.

One day I received an e-mail from a teacher in Washington State. She'd learned of my project through a memo circulated by the Washington Teachers Association. Her name was Peggy Hotes, and her note read:

> My very good friend, Elaine Moore, recently retired from elementary teaching in Eagle River, Alaska. Elaine was an outstanding and compassionate teacher. One year a fourth-grade student of hers was diagnosed with terminal brain cancer. Elaine organized her class into small groups who would visit the student every day at home to keep him involved in what was going on at school. . . . There is much more to the story than I can relay in this message.

I called Peggy Hotes. She furnished a few details beyond what was written in her note and urged me, if I found this to be an appropriate story, to follow up by speaking directly with her friend. Peggy did warn me that Elaine Moore was exceedingly modest and would probably be quick to downplay her role. "She's an amazing person," Peggy explained, "but she doesn't think of herself that way."

This last detail certainly rang true. I'd interviewed many teachers. In addition, I'd gotten to know quite a few of the wonderful teachers my sons have been blessed to have during their years of schooling. By and large, teachers are smart, worldly, professional, articulate, self-assured.

What they generally are not is boastful, hyperbolic,

self-aggrandizing, opportunistic (except when it comes to seizing those famed "teachable moments"). Teachers do not tend to be the sort of preening, chest-thumping, fist-waving braggarts that disproportionately occupy center stage in our prime-time media arenas. Nor, I should add, do they go to great lengths to cloak themselves in the aw-shucks faux humility that is its own form of hustle.

So I was not surprised to hear that Elaine Moore might not greet me with a full-blown zeal for self-exposure. I phoned Elaine, introduced myself, and explained my reason for calling and how she'd come to my attention. Elaine was polite and predictably reserved. She did acknowledge that some years ago a remarkable series of events had occurred in her class related to a student who was diagnosed with terminal cancer. I asked her to please tell me more about it.

And so she did. Elaine told me in easy, clear, unassuming language about the year her class of fourth graders made a valiant effort to keep a bedridden classmate up to speed with his schoolwork, even though they knew he was soon going to die. I asked why. "Because the kids knew school meant so much to him," Elaine matter-of-factly explained.

We spoke that first time for half an hour. On several occasions as Elaine was telling me about that year, tears sprang to my eyes. I'd phoned her in search of an uplifting incident, and now I was crying. I thought to myself: this is not a simple story.

I have now interviewed many of Elaine's former fourth graders, who are now college age, as well as most of the grown-ups intimately involved in the events of that year. They do not all remember it in the same way, but they certainly all remember it.

Something special happened in a fourth-grade class in Eagle River, Alaska. To hear Elaine tell it with her characteristic modesty, it was just a unique set of circumstances that coincided to bring out the best in a lot of people, including the children. There's something to that. But those unique circumstances, I've come to understand, were to a great extent created by a unique teacher with a special regard for a concept we like to admire from afar but have largely lost the knack for putting into practice: community.

As Elaine Moore and her fourth graders demonstrated, community involves more than convenient rhetoric. It's a process, a method, a practice, an outlook, a perspective. It has no beginning and no end. It is a circle.

· 1 ·

ELAINE'S VOICE

When she first trained to become a schoolteacher, Elaine Moore was warned that her voice would be her one big liability. Her voice was soft, languid, unaffected. Elaine's was a voice that soothed and made no demands. It was a comforting pillow of a voice, familiar and reassuring. It was a background murmur of a voice rather than a center-stage announcement kind of voice. The flat enunciations of her prairie upbringing in rural Manitoba lent her voice the steadiness of a distant horizon. If Elaine's voice fluctuated at all, it was in the direction of less urgency, not more. Over time, the voice might relax a listener into an unsuspecting and delightful nap. You could imagine professional hypnotists striving hard to imitate such a voice. But of course their objectives—to tranquilize, to desensitize, to reduce consciousness—would be the exact opposite of a good schoolteacher's.

It was no mystery why Elaine's education professors at Brandon College and her mentor teachers expressed concern about her voice. They worried that rambunctious youngsters would run roughshod over anyone who tried to command a classroom using such mild tones. They worried that kids would drown her out with their noisy carryings-on. They worried that the fragile decorum that teachers try so assiduously to maintain would constantly be at risk in a classroom where kids had difficulty even hearing what the teacher was saying, never mind obeying her message. They were concerned, quite simply, that Elaine's voice—quiet, patient, charitable—might precipitate every school system's worst-case scenario: out-and-out mayhem. It had been known to occur.

But that's not what happened. Instead, Elaine's voice, which she could no more alter than can a songbird, turned out to be her greatest asset. Students in rear seats straining to hear what she had to say did not revolt. They did not mock the timidity and self-effacement normally associated with such a voice. They did not engage in the maddeningly ingenious things kids often do when they sense weakness or peculiarity in an authority figure. They did not resort to the deviousness of using the questionable audibility of her voice as a blanket excuse for just about everything, from botched homework assignments ("I thought you said it was due next week") to lingering too long at recess. Her students did not use her soft-spoken quality as a license for slipshod work or for insurrection.

Instead, Elaine's voice achieved a very different result. The children perked up. They hushed. They leaned forward. They were intrigued to know what this teacher who comported herself with none of the typical stagecraft of professional instructors had to say. They simmered to an immaculate silence. How else be certain to hear every word?

On the other hand, her voice did not always have the right effect with adults. Her gentleness and understated whimsy did not always command grown-up respect. As a result, Elaine often found that she could be her fullest, truest self only in the company of children. They had fewer preconceptions than adults, and they were not in such a hurry. Standing up and speaking before a roomful of adults struck her as a grim and daunting prospect. A roomful of children was the pond she was meant to swim in.

Elaine Moore's manner of speaking was slow, thoughtful, musical. Her words had texture and pitch. They had timbre and melody and an almost palpable shape. They were objects. They held color and weight. They were autumn leaves gliding on invisible currents. To speak hurriedly would amount almost to an act of sabotage. Data output to comply with deadline pressures was the only reason to hurry. Data output was decidedly not how Elaine viewed the mission of being a teacher.

Elaine was careful about her choice of words, and just as

careful about the silences between them. Pauses were not empty spaces. They were anything but. Pauses could be dynamic and exciting. The right kind of pause was a veritable beehive of unseen mental activity. Pauses between words were like the intermissions in a good play, allowing the theatergoer time to consider the busy preparations taking place backstage, and what might happen next. Pauses meant anticipation. Pauses were dramatic interludes. Pauses enhanced the surrounding notes. Pauses were communication.

Above all, Elaine wanted her students to have an abiding respect for learning—and an appreciation for words was fundamental to this goal. Addressing her class, Elaine was an artist—a term, incidentally, she would never, ever use to describe herself—and she demonstrated a true artist's desire to bring her audience into her sensibility. Soft words spoken slowly, woven into stories and conversation, and dispensed with affection—that was Elaine Moore's art. The kids, of course, knew only that they were in class with a teacher who really cared.

They circled around her as she sat among them. With forefingers pressed to pursed lips, the children would shush each other to hasten the moment when Elaine would begin. The chatter would subside. The playful jostling would come to a halt. The squirming arms and legs of exuberant bodies would gradually retract. A passerby gazing from the school corridor might mistake the group for a concert audience who'd paid a steep ticket price doing its best to show the soloist onstage that they were finally ready.

The crowd faces forward. The soloist nods. The show begins.

Elaine loved to tell stories to her kids. These stories were not the kind that normally captivate grade-schoolers. They were not fantasies or fictions or tales of legendary figures or neatly wrapped parables capped by edifying homilies. They were mostly just tales drawn from her own experience, accounts of events that had occurred to her or to her family or close friends—which she possessed in ever-expanding numbers. The story might involve a wicked teacher she had had when she was a girl in a one-room farm community schoolhouse, or her younger brother Ron's exploits as a competitive curler (yes, curler!), or the German prisoners of war housed on her farm, or the black bear that had started making itself comfortable beneath her side deck. There was not much deliberation to these stories. The words were improvised, the flow was improvised, and the points of emphasis depended on a host of variables, including topics they were studying in class, events in the world at large, the weather front swooping into the valley just outside the big glass windows of their classroom. Strangely, Elaine rarely knew she was going to launch into a story until the moment arose. Then, suddenly, she was telling it, and twenty-six eager faces tilted toward her, hanging on her every word.

For a woman of an almost congenital modesty that had led her to conclude, wrongly, that most other people lived far more dramatic lives and therefore had far more impor- tant things to say, this penchant for storytelling was a bit surprising. Elaine herself had not even known it was in her. She'd always been the perfect listener. She'd listened, rapt, to the flowing and convoluted tales told by her father and mother and especially by her older sister, who could spin out stories so irresistible and fraught with dizzying twists and turns that family members in a hurry to get somewhere on time made a point of avoiding her lest they get snagged for an hour they did not have to spare. Her sister Norma was the storyteller. Elaine certainly never thought of herself that way.

Until she became a teacher. Then, something clicked. As with all magical occurrences, it was probably a confluence of factors—the forgiving nature of children, the special license in having a captive audience that was hers alone, subtle developments in her own emerging sense of self—that contributed to the transformation. But transformation was certainly the word for it. Seemingly overnight, Elaine went from being an undemonstrative woman with a nearly inaudible voice and a habitual urge to dodge attention into a mesmerizing showstopper who constantly left a roomful of fresh-faced youngsters pleading impatiently, "Please, please, Mrs. Moore. Please, tell us more!"

2

HOLIDAY ON ICE

R avenwood School, where Elaine Moore taught, is
tucked in a steep valley close to the rushing waters of
Eagle River and the dark mountain rising above it. In these
northern latitudes, where in late June it's light enough at
3 AM to read a book outdoors, there are but a few hours of
sunlight in the winter months. Children arrive at school in
darkness and often depart in it as well. For safety, the Ravenwood grounds are illuminated by bright floodlights affixed
to tall poles, lending the scene the stage-lit appearance of a
lunar landing pad in a sci-fi movie.

Located fifteen miles north of Anchorage on the edge
of a vast wilderness beneath towering glacial peaks, Eagle
River often gets its first snowfall by mid-October. By

mid-December, everything flat and most things slanted are coated in thick layers of brilliant white—the borders of the parking lot behind Joy Lutheran Church, the fenced-in yards of the upscale homes in the Eaglewood subdivision, the gravel skirt surrounding the makeshift drive-up coffee shacks along Old Glenn Highway, the winding paths of the nature center at the end of Eagle River Road.

Holiday season in Eagle River never fails to deliver a picture-postcard winter wonderland. With church steeples, tree limbs, hillsides, and roadsides cloaked in deep drifts of snow, a white Christmas is pretty much guaranteed. No need to tune in to one of the ritual TV reruns of *It's a Wonderful Life* to get an eyeful of what a small community nestled in mounds of snow actually looks like. It is everywhere you turn.

In December, schoolchildren in Eagle River begin their morning in darkness so complete it is indistinguishable from the dead of night. Children at bus stops shiver and squint half-blind into the headlights of oncoming cars. Yellow buses crusty with road salt downshift from the hills and cautiously come to a halt. Youngsters, some needing a boost, climb aboard. Sitting on lumpy vinyl-covered seats, they press their faces to frosted windows. The bus rolls by roadside homesteads embroidered with twinkling Christmas lights strung in ornate tracings of gutters, fences, doorways, bushes, and the occasional wire outline of reindeer and sleigh.

At Ravenwood Elementary, the buses pull into the semi-circular driveway. Kids, more awake now, scramble off, spilling across the floodlit school yard. Behind Ravenwood is a sledding hill. Some children, having arrived early, can be seen merrily whisking down. In a few minutes, the morning bell will ring. Teachers bundled in winter coats wait by the front door, beckoning them inside. The children have arrived at a place that is safe and warm.

Ravenwood Elementary is a one-story building of stucco-covered cinder block, built in 1985. It serves grades K–6 and houses some six hundred students. The school has an airy (due to its high ceilings), amiable, child-friendly feel. The walls are a vanilla shade with green trim. The linoleum floor is a speckled light brown, easy to clean and capable of camouflaging minor amounts of dirt. Almost everyone along the hallway, kids and adults, has a bounce in their step, and at least a hint of a smile. When the sun is out, it floods through the school's numerous skylights and banks of windows.

Ravenwood's long corridors of classrooms branch off a central nexus that contains the multipurpose room (cafeteria, school assemblies, and anything else requiring a large gathering), a gymnasium, and what amounts to the school's nerve center, the suite of offices housing the principal, the school secretaries, and the nurse. It is from here that periodic public-address announcements are issued, warning children on their way home to be on the watch for a bear or moose lurking near certain bus stops.

Ravenwood is a very parent-friendly school. There are no

stringent security restrictions, and parents are welcomed as classroom volunteers or helpers in the library. People seem to know each other. Custodians nod to mothers dropping off left-behind lunches. Dads picking up kids for a doctor's checkup are greeted by name by the central office staff. There is an in-house PTA office directly across from the school office, where parents can gather to discuss Ravenwood activities or team up for organizational tasks like the Thanksgiving canned-food drive.

• • •

On December 18, 1992, two days before Christmas break, the Ravenwood School office was busy fielding absentee calls from parents. A virulent flu had been going around, and Debbie Corral, the school nurse, was advising parents whose kids showed symptoms to please stay home. This preholiday week of celebrations, with plates of homemade cookies clutched and crumbled and shared by busy hands, could only hasten the spread of germs and aggravate the situation.

Beyond the central office lay the faculty lounge, the library, the Occupational and Physical Therapy room, and the music, art, bilingual, and speech resource rooms. Elaine Moore's fourth-grade class was near the center of one of the two corridors. The shape of her room, Room 112, was a standard rectangle, yet a casual observer would have been forgiven for construing it as wildly, even eccentrically asymmetrical. The shelf space overflowed with plastic tubs crammed with art supplies, bins containing feathers and fossils, skulls and bones, a fish tank, a guinea-pig cage, a wasps' nest, a gyrating globe, and books, books, and more books. Nearly every square inch of wall space was covered by a dizzying array of drawings, maps, writings, posters, helpful-hint aphorisms (LEARNING IS FUN!!). Elaine loved filling her room up with stuff. The saddest day of every year for her was generally the day in June after school let out, when it was time to pack it all away.

Elaine was fifty years old, and this was her fifteenth full year of teaching. A rosy-complexioned, red-haired, spirited woman, Elaine managed to tastefully combine several traits that would seem contradictory in a less composed person.

She was both high-energy and serene. She was tireless, but never hyper. She was agreeable, yet possessed an iron will. She was shy, yet had a flair for free-association story-telling. Her regular output—teaching twenty-five children, raising three daughters, volunteering for worthwhile civic functions—bespoke someone of enormous drive and determination. Yet she was singularly unambitious, at least in any standard sense.

First and foremost, Elaine was a teacher. The question of where she got all her energy, or what inspired her to even try to accomplish so much, was, to her, beside the point. Her point was simply that there were things that had to get done.

She had a rare ability to be considered the single-most-trusted friend to many. "Other than my husband, she's the only person I called when I went into labor," recalled teaching colleague Peggy Hotes. To her many friends and colleagues, Elaine was renowned for a kind of stalwart pleasantness, even when irked (an emotion you had to know her quite well to detect). Her unflagging optimism could sometimes be grating. But only if you did not share her abiding belief that bad things often yielded unexpected good. Even her untimely divorce was a development Elaine was sure, once the initial trauma subsided, would deliver its benefits. At least that's what she told people. And told herself.

• • •

On this morning, Elaine stood at the window of Room 112, waiting for the kids to file in. She gazed out across the floodlit expanse of playground and the adjoining ice rink, where at recess she could see the heads of children, visible above the sideboards, gliding up and around, back and around. She could not see their scooting feet. She could not hear the harsh scrape of steel blades on hard ice. From Room 112, all she could see were their thickly cloaked torsos and faces topped with stocking caps, gliding like motorized figurines in a tinsel-strewn store-window holiday diorama.

These final days before Christmas break were normally the happiest of times. Elaine loved celebrations, and if the calendar were hers to fashion, it would be crammed with them. She loved celebrations for the structure and predictability they imprinted on the shapelessness that spilled across normal weeks and months. She loved celebrations for the pause they imposed on the blur of life. And there was nothing quite like the Christmas holiday—all that good cheer coupled with an actual two-week vacation.

No, there never was a right time for gloomy news, but today, with the festive all-school holiday pageant scheduled for the afternoon, had to be about the worst.

Elaine turned away from the window. Her students were starting to filter in. They tugged off their caps and stuffed them in the sleeves of their bulky parkas. They were a chattering, boisterous group, all the more so with the onset of the holiday. Two more days until break! Had she not been so disturbed by the call she'd received the night before, Elaine would have been as gleeful as the kids.

• • •

The night before, Elaine had been at home packing for her long-awaited trip to Australia to visit her daughter Leigh Anne and brand-new grandchild. "I'd hoped she would marry a doctor or lawyer," was about as far as Elaine would go toward expressing regret that Leigh Anne lived so far away, "but she married a surfer instead."

While hunting through dresser drawers for items she'd need in the Down Under weather (where had she put her shorts? her bathing suit?), Elaine had received a phone call from Susan Farrell, the mother of one of her students.

Elaine always gave parents her home number, and it wasn't uncommon for parents to call her. In fact, she encouraged it.

Susan Farrell's voice on the phone was sweet and straightforward, with mild tonal hints of her native Bronx, New York. She apologized for phoning so late, but she needed to talk. Elaine assured her it was fine.

From the very outset of the school year, Seamus Farrell had caught Elaine's eye. He had bright blue eyes and dark brown hair that went sandy-colored under the summer sun and whorled crazily around multiple cowlicks. He was energetic, nimble, enthusiastic, a lover of the outdoors. He was high-spirited and popular with the other kids, girls as well as boys. He was the type of headfirst diver into life who always seemed to have a scrape or a bruise or a smudge somewhere on his thin frame.

Seamus was, in Elaine's words, "all boy," and by that she meant no criticism. She genuinely loved boys. Raising three daughters, she said, had left her curious about what it would be like to raise a son. Like everything about Elaine, there was probably more to it.

In fact, she was known for her success in teaching boys, especially the notoriously difficult ones. According to Joan Johnson, an earthy fourth-grade teacher who'd studied drama at Central Washington University and retained the leading-lady looks of the actress she might have become, "They knew they could be who they were with her. Elaine loved the devilish, untamed spirit in boys. She never wanted to break that spirit. She only wanted to help them tame it."

There were many reasons Seamus had caught Elaine's eye, but the primary one was that he was precisely the type of student she found most challenging, and interesting, to teach.

Seamus was not a fast or efficient learner. He was not a natural at pen and paperwork. He was a capable reader, but not zealous about book assignments. Math concepts could sometimes befuddle him. But unlike some boys who react to schoolwork difficulties with a macho shrug, pretending it really doesn't matter, Seamus was always eager to learn. He would, in Elaine's words, "just burst through the door every morning, raring to go." It was as if this boy were announcing, "Here I am! What're we gonna do today?"

There was never any doubt that he was bright. Indeed, Elaine operated on the assumption that most kids are innately bright. The only questions were: Could she find a way to effectively teach him? Could she succeed well enough to allow him to succeed? That's how she viewed her mission. All children were inherent learners; it was the teacher's job to figure out how to make it happen. "With Elaine," Joan Johnson noted, "there was never, *ever* a 'throwaway' child."

When Susan Farrell phoned, Elaine took the call in her kitchen. Her house, a modest A-frame, sat on a hill that would command a majestic view to the river were it not for the thicket of cottonwoods lower down the slope.

Elaine assumed Susan was calling to say that Seamus

would miss the final days before break. He'd missed most of the past couple of weeks because of the flu, with the same symptoms of vomiting, dehydration, and fever that were affecting so many other kids. Seamus's illness was unusual only in that it had lasted longer than the other kids'. He was the type of effervescent sprite whose absence was always noticed, even with twenty-five rambunctious, attention-grabbing classmates to fill the void.

Susan came right to the point. Seamus, she said, had a brain tumor.

Elaine gasped. It took her a moment to get her bearings.

The discovery, Susan explained, had come about without warning, and the family was still reeling. Dehydrated from what they'd believed was merely a nasty flu, Seamus was now being hurriedly prepped by IV feedings to strengthen him for surgery. The surgery was to take place first thing tomorrow morning.

"How is he doing?"

"You know Seamus," Susan said. After a pause, she added, "I think he's worried."

Susan's voice, Elaine thought, sounded firm. If there was an undercurrent of trepidation, Elaine didn't know her well enough to detect it. Back in October, Susan had not been able to attend her parent-teacher conference. Instead, it was her husband, Jim, who'd come. A tough yet affable Alaska state trooper whose hobby was reading history books, Jim had listened thoughtfully to Elaine's evaluation of Seamus ("struggles in some areas," "approaches every task eagerly"), but said little. That was often the case with dads, unless they had a specific issue to discuss.

At the conference, Jim was not surprised to hear that his son had a few academic shortcomings. What surprised him was how unabashedly Seamus sought his teacher's approval. (Elaine insisted that her students not only be present at, but actually *lead*, the parent conferences; it was a way to prod the kids into taking responsibility for their own learning. If a more private session was needed, that would come later.) According to Jim, "Whenever Ms. Moore said anything, you could just tell that Seamus really, *really* wanted it to be praise."

As the conference wound down, Elaine pulled Jim aside. She wanted to bring to his attention the fact that Seamus had a slight limp, which she'd been noticing for weeks. On some days it was worse than others. "He tells me it's just something he did to his ankle playing football," Elaine reported, clearly skeptical.

Jim shook his head and chuckled. "That's our Seamus. Told *us* he fell off the jungle gym."

● ● ●

Susan Farrell continued filling Elaine in on the alarming sequence of events. As Seamus's headaches and vomiting intensified, Susan had finally taken him to see his pediatrician, Dr. Ron Keller. In the elevator ride up to the doctor's office, Susan heard a thump and turned to see Seamus slumped on the floor. He quickly hopped to his feet, laughing. When they got in to see the doctor, Susan immediately told him that Seamus had fainted.

Seamus corrected her. "I didn't faint, Mommy. I just fell down."

"And his ankle's been sore for weeks," Susan added before Seamus could cut her off.

Dr. Keller made note of this. But it was the flu they were here to have treated. He prescribed an antinausea drug to quell the vomiting.

The drug had no appreciable effect. Seamus grew steadily weaker. Again, Susan took him to see the doctor. Puzzled by the boy's deterioration, Keller reviewed the file. He considered the lingering ankle problem as well as the report of the elevator collapse. Although neither seemed related to the vomiting, and each was dismissed by Seamus with a simple explanation, Dr. Keller thought it prudent to explore further. With a flat stainless steel instrument, he grazed the underside of Seamus's foot.

Susan held her breath. In the fall, she'd entered nursing school on a part-time basis, and this procedure was one she had recently learned. She knew exactly what the doctor was doing. And why. As the doctor's instrument traced the tender bottom of his foot, Seamus's big toe lifted as his other toes shot outward. In a very young child, less than two years old, this particular reflex action was considered normal. But in older children or adults, the type of stimulus Dr. Keller was applying should have caused the toes to turn downward.

Susan was shocked. This reaction, she had just learned, was indicative of neurological problems, with a suggestion of damage to the nerve paths connecting the spinal cord and the brain. Susan even knew the medical term for it, Babinski reflex, named after the French neurologist who'd discovered it.

Dr. Keller did not disclose his own conjecture, if he had one. He only said that Seamus needed a CAT scan, and he wanted it performed immediately. He told Susan there was no time to spare.

•   •   •

"Seamus really wanted me to tell you about this," Susan informed Elaine, winding down her account. "He cares so much about the class."

"Yes," Elaine sighed. "I know."

"It just means the world to him," Susan continued. "He talks about you and the kids all the time."

Elaine knew that that was true. The class meant a lot to Seamus, and to all her students. Caring about classmates and belonging to the group was precisely the behavior Elaine had been cultivating these past months. Beyond the math, the reading, the science, the grammar, Elaine wanted her students to learn that they were part of a community. She wanted them to experience the sharing and the intimacy and the trust that can develop in a group. She wanted them to experience the joys of belonging, really belonging. She wanted them to understand that the learning they struggled so hard to achieve had a purpose, and the purpose was to help not just themselves, but also others.

This notion of learning—that it is first and foremost something you do in concert with others, that it must be *social*—was not especially in vogue. A sense of community was not an item on the curriculum. Neither the school board nor the principal would hand out certificates of achievement for it. No tests would be given on the topic—at least none that could be graded or assigned a numerical score. At a time when the pressure was mounting to spend more and more classroom time on the designated core curriculum, i.e., material that would appear on the battery of standardized tests by which the school district, the principal, and the school faculty would be judged, Elaine was something close to a rebel.

She had been known to interrupt a lesson on a winter's afternoon because there was an astonishing glint of sunlight on a mound of snow across the playground. The entire class would be asked to stop what they were doing and go to the window, just to quietly look.

Other teachers at Ravenwood were surprised, and not always approvingly so, that Elaine would spend precious class time on what appeared to them to be nothing more than sitting on the floor and talking.

But this "sitting on the floor and talking" was Circle Time, and the time she and the children spent at it was absolutely crucial to Elaine's mission—which was nothing less, she felt, than preparing kids for life.

At the start of every school year, Elaine introduced her new crop of fourth graders to a book entitled *I'm in Charge of Celebrations*. The author, Byrd Baylor, portrays a young girl, possibly Native American, who inhabits a desert landscape of hills and canyons with no visible neighbors. The girl is asked if she gets lonely living in such an environment. "How can I be lonely?" the girl wonders to herself. "I'm the one in charge of celebrations."

The book describes how the girl turns common happenings in the world around her into causes for celebration. There's Dust Devil Day, which celebrates the whirlwinds that rush through the ravines. There's Coyote Day, September 28, commemorating a surprise encounter with a coyote that stopped in its tracks to stare at the girl like she "was just another creature following another rocky trail." The girl even has her own New Year's Day—not January 1, but a day on the cusp of spring, "when winter ends and morning light comes earlier. . . . That's when I feel like starting new."

Elaine wanted her kids to think about which occurrences in their lives could qualify as the stuff of a brand-new celebration. That's how she wanted them to view the ebb and flow of every day.

She would ask them, "Who has a day you can turn into a celebration?"

The kids would gush forth with suggestions.

A boy had seen a moose at the bus stop.

"What was special about it?"

The boy scratched his scalp, thinking. "It just kind of stood there."

"Yes. And?"

"It looked like it was just waiting there till we got on the bus. Like a parent."

So that one became Mama Moose at the Bus Stop Day. Her classes came up with First Salmon in Russian River Day, and Freak Snow in September Day.

Elaine was a lover of traditions and an avid inventor of new ones. The past, she believed, has great virtues. But that is no reason to leave it untouched.

Dubious colleagues would saunter by Elaine's room in hopes of glimpsing the chaos they felt would surely result from giving students so much leeway. Mostly, they were disappointed. Elaine stood before the children, speaking in her soft, steady voice. "You could," according to one teacher, "hear a pin drop."

And Seamus Farrell, this lively sprite who was always willing to hazard a guess and never got discouraged, was, in Elaine's view, a veritable poster child for everything she was trying to accomplish as a teacher. No, it did not surprise her to hear that Seamus had insisted that his mother call from the hospital to let Mrs. Moore and the kids know about the trouble he was in. It didn't surprise her at all.

• • •

There was one other crucial detail that Susan told Elaine

about the surgery. Seamus's tumor, as evidenced by the MRI, was large. It measured approximately 5 centimeters by 4 centimeters and appeared to be at least partially embedded in the right hemisphere of his brain. When she was told this, Susan, knowing too much, doubled over. The doctor, awkwardly trying to calm her, had yammered on about cell mitosis and then had gone off on some tangent about the Irish Republican Army that had seemed lunatic to her, as did all considerations outside her son's predicament at that horrible moment.

When Susan regained equilibrium, the doctor explained that he would not know exactly what they were dealing with until they had "opened him up." It was a chilling yet accurate phrase. The doctors expected that they would know fairly early in the process. There was a chance—there is always a chance—that the MRI had misled them about certain details. That, too, would be quickly determined. But until they could closely inspect the tumor, they would not know if it could be removed—removed, that is, without risking damage to Seamus's brain.

In other words, the longer the surgery lasted, the more likely it was that the surgeons were meeting with success, the more likely that Seamus's tumor was indeed operable. A prompt conclusion to the surgery would indicate that nothing could be done.

From what Susan gathered, the optimal time frame for the surgery would be around eight hours. It would take approximately an hour and a half just to prepare Seamus's skull, including the cutting through to the brain. It would take another hour, or more, to close him up. The procedure would begin before 9 AM. Doing the math was not the hard part. The waiting would be the hard part.

• • •

Circle Time was the emotional centerpiece of Elaine's teaching style. Each morning, immediately after attendance was taken and Ravenwood's principal had wrapped up his announcements over the PA system, Elaine would move to the center of the room. Like a camp counselor urging everyone into the pool, she'd say, "Circle up."

Kids hopped from their desks to take up positions on the carpet. It only worked, Elaine knew, if everyone sat together on the floor. Over the years, Elaine had been assigned several student teachers from the University of Alaska, eager young collegians diligently studying the craft of professional teaching.

"Does it really have to be the floor?" they'd squeamishly ask.

"Yes," she'd insist. "You need intimacy to reach children. Sit with them on the floor."

Initially, Circle Time was awkward for some of the kids. They were not always comfortable sharing their thoughts and feelings in a group setting. Some felt they had nothing to say, at least nothing that could hold the attention of their antsy classmates. Others were simply shy. But Elaine had her ways around such difficulties.

She might ask the kids to turn to their "shoulder buddy," the child seated nearest them on the floor, and conduct an interview, after which they would report to the class at least one interesting detail they had learned.

"She's been to Disney World!"

"His uncle caught a halibut bigger than he was!"

A surefire way to loosen them up was with tales from her own prairie girlhood. Like the bitter March afternoon when she and her brother Rae, five and six years old respectively, decided to have an adventure.

"Dad always had a nap after lunch," Elaine began. "Many farmers did, since they wake up so early and work so hard. So we knew if we waited until Dad's nap we could go down to the slough . . ."

"What's a 'slough,' Mrs. Moore?"

"It's like a pond. We went there because Rae had just got a new pair of rubber boots, which was a rare and prized possession. The slough was all iced over and Rae's shiny new boots were perfect for sliding. So we went sliding out on the glistening sheet of newly frozen ice. Suddenly, the middle fell through. At first, we were just having a great time, bobbing around in the water. Then we started breaking the ice, thinking we could just break our way back to shore. But the ice became too thick. We couldn't break our way out. It got really cold. We started to get worried."

Elaine had the class's attention now! She told them how she glanced at Rae and he looked back at her. Her brother looked uncertain. His shiny black boots had filled with water, and it was hard for him to move. Rae took the boots off and placed them side by side on top of the ice. Elaine's homemade woolen leggings and coat had become soaked and were very heavy. The frigid water was over their heads, but they managed to hang onto the lip of ice. The scariest part, scarier than the hurt, was when the hurt just vanished, when the cold on her face and submerged limbs stopped being cold. She turned to her brother, who was one year older and would surely know how to get out of this mess, and he looked as worried as her. She tried to yell to her mother and father. No words came out. She'd lost her voice in the gathering cold.

Well, that was the start of just one of the stories Elaine told the kids. She wanted to show them that in Circle Time, you could talk about anything, so long as it had meaning for you. It didn't have to be about school. It didn't have to be about something earth-shaking or topical. But it had to connect to something they cared about, something they could consider writing about during Writers' Workshop, which came later in the morning.

Elaine had to be careful that her riveting tales not set too daunting a standard. So she might start by getting them talking about their pets. Or she might ask if anyone had noticed the constellations in the sky last night. Anything to get it flowing. She pointed out that what she had told them was a "Remember when" story. Every family has such tales, she said, and the tale often begins, "Remember when . . ."

A circle, Elaine explained, has no beginning and no end.

Native American groups recognize the power of the circle. It is a universal symbol of wholeness. The circle exists throughout our world in many manifestations, if we only know where to look.

She'd ask children to offer examples of circles in their lives.

"The wheel."

"The change of seasons."

"The globe, there on the shelf."

In a circle of people, Elaine pointed out, rotating her gaze around the circumference of the group, each person is able to see everyone else. "When someone is absent from our circle," she said, "our circle has an empty space in it."

There had been a lot of empty spaces recently, with the flu affecting so many. Seamus Farrell's absence was notable only for its length and for the fact that he was such an irrepressible participant in Circle Time.

Elaine had two ironclad rules for Circle Time: anyone could say whatever he or she wanted, so long as it had some connection to learning and nobody was allowed to criticize or scorn another's remarks. A boy could say he was mad at his brother for ruining his Lego construction. A child could talk about losing a favorite mitten, if it tied in to a lesson or discussion. Or a girl could say, as little Grace did one morning, that her father had committed suicide over the weekend and she felt it was her fault because he was always angry with her.

Elaine wondered what grown-ups who knew nothing of elementary school norms would make of this. Most adults, she believed, would, if allowed to eavesdrop, be astounded at how sensitive, articulate, thoughtful, and wise ten-year-olds can be. Circle Time was like watching a movie that never stopped being interesting, and never failed to enrich. At least, that's how it was for her.

A movie, by the way, in which she was determined not to act as director. Elaine sat in the circle as one of them. Not at the head (for a circle has none), nor at the center. When a pupil finished speaking, Elaine might commend him or her by noting, "That would sure make a great story."

Stories were instrumental—hers and theirs. Stories were circles—perhaps not in a geometric sense, but in the way that they enveloped all who were touched by them, including the narrator. Once the kids grew familiar with the process, they were the ones who'd leap to congratulate a classmate, declaring, "Wow! That's so cool! You should write about that!"

The key to making Circle Time work, in Elaine's estimation, was making sure that the children were committed to the process of talking, listening, and respecting each other. "You can't just put people in a group and call it a community," she liked to say.

Once, in a fit of self-doubt, Elaine asked Joan Johnson, "Do you think I'm devoting too much time to Circle Time?"

"Well, what are the benefits?" Joan asked. "What would happen if you took it away?"

"Well . . ." Elaine stammered. "Well . . . we simply couldn't function."

"What do you mean, you couldn't function?"

"If I took it away, we'd just be doing bookwork. We'd just be filling in blanks. That's not enough."

• • •

Incidentally, Elaine's story about falling through the ice did not end with her hollering for help to no avail. For several minutes, she and Rae struggled. They took turns trying to boost each other atop the cracking ice, but neither had the strength to successfully haul the other up after them. With the situation growing desperate, it was agreed that Elaine would be hoisted out and make a dash for the farmhouse to fetch their father.

"Dad had awakened from his nap," she told the kids. "He was out looking for us and I could hear him calling. But I couldn't answer. I opened my mouth and nothing came out."

Finally, Elaine's father spotted her. Barely able to move in her water-logged woolen leggings, she stumbled toward him. He screamed, "Where's Rae?" Unable to speak, Elaine pointed to the pond. Her father lit into a sprint, hurdling the cattle fence with his lead leg straight out. Her mother took her inside and stripped off her clothes.

Suddenly, her father burst through the door carrying her brother in his outstretched arms. Rae's head lolled back and his face was a ghastly blue. Her mother whipped the oilcloth off the dining table, sending her precious china heirloom cream salt and pepper shakers crashing to the floor. Her parents began furiously rubbing Rae's body with warming liniment, desperately trying to rub the life back into him. After a full hour, a recognizable pulse was finally restored.

"We didn't wake up until the next day," Elaine told the kids. "And guess what? We didn't get yelled at. Instead, we were treated like royalty. Mom and Dad were laughing and laughing. They were just giddy. Then when Rae was well enough, Dad took us into town for a five-cent vanilla ice cream cone. It was the one and only time we were ever given ice cream outside of summer."

"So Rae and I got to thinking"—and here Elaine cracked a smile to acknowledge that yes, peril can sometimes have an unforeseen flip side—"maybe this falling through the ice wasn't such a bad idea after all."

• • •

"Circle up," Elaine announced.

The kids were a bit more boisterous than usual. On this, the second to last day before break, there would not be much formal schoolwork. It took them a minute to calm down. Elaine raised her hand, signaling that she wanted to speak. She had given a great deal of thought to what to say. She did not want to spoil the holiday mood. But it was crucial that the children know about Seamus.

"You're aware," she told them, "that Seamus has been sick for the past couple of weeks."

They nodded knowingly. More than a third of them had been out with the flu at one time or another.

"Last night I spoke to his mother. Some of you know Mrs. Farrell."

The jostling and sly games of footsie quickly came to a halt.

"Seamus has a brain tumor," Elaine said. "It's a very serious thing. Should I explain what that is?"

The children nodded again.

Elaine gave a brief description, minus any medical jargon. A tumor was a growth, but not the kind that you wanted or that would do you any good. While no tumors were good, some were very, very dangerous. If a tumor grew big enough, it could interfere with the part of the body where it was located. She asked what they knew about the brain and its importance. A few hands went up.

"It runs the body."

"It makes your decisions."

"Like a computer, sort of, in your head."

"Where smarts come from."

"Yes," Elaine said. "You're all right. The brain, along with your heart, is probably your most vital organ."

She tried to imagine how the children perceived this information. The actual physiology might elude some of them. But the fact that their classmate was in very serious trouble would not.

"Seamus is having surgery this morning, at Providence Medical Center in Anchorage," she told them. "His mother said he really wanted you to know about it."

"Right now?" one student asked. "He's having surgery right now?"

Elaine checked the clock on the wall. "Yes, right now," she answered.

None of the kids moved. Elaine could almost see the children's thoughts bounding to the hospital with Seamus. They were making that huge empathetic leap that was breathtaking, even inspiring, to behold.

Finally one boy asked, "Is it from the flu?"

Elaine saw where this might lead. "No, it has nothing to do with the flu."

"But he's had the flu really bad."

"It's not related to the flu," Elaine assured them.

A girl asked, "Can he die from it?"

Elaine had observed that kids can often sense when an adult is holding something back. They intuit it from body language, vocal manner, eye movement, biochemical signals—who knows? But somehow, some way, they know. Therefore, she believed you must be as forthright with them as you possibly can. Teachers who challenged Elaine on this point would always come up with hypotheticals—what if this, what if that—and Elaine readily agreed that there were many facts that were far too upsetting to dump in the laps of ten-year-olds. She was not an absolutist. She allowed that there were some truths that ought properly to be withheld from children. But in her opinion, the medical plight, no matter how bleak, of a classmate was not one of those things. Kids, she believed, can handle most truths.

What most frightens them is *not knowing.* She'd been there. She knew.

"Yes," Elaine told them. "Seamus could die from this."

There were audible gasps.

"But we hope he doesn't."

"But in the hospital they're helping him, right?" another girl added hopefully.

It was soon to be Christmas. Elaine saw no reason to dampen their obvious wish that Seamus's misfortune come to a happy conclusion, like her ice pond story.

"That's right," Elaine answered, glancing again at the clock. "The doctors are doing their very best to help him."

Elaine did, however, elect not to disclose one fact about Seamus's surgery: the longer it lasted, the better were his prospects. That was an example of the type of information that could do the kids no good; it would only wreak havoc on their day. As it was doing to hers.

• • •

At around 10 AM, she packed them off to the music room for a last rehearsal of this year's holiday program.

Gray light tinged with violet pushed into the valley. Dawn was creeping in. To Elaine, who felt an almost moral obligation to be maximally attentive to nature's wonders, it was always a treat to experience dawn in this deep valley. The outdoor floodlights muted some of its effect, but Elaine knew where to look. Across the playground, toward the peak of the dark mountain behind the river, above the tree line—that's where you could see the subtle play of the first light, little hints of rouge on that jutting black cliff side.

Elaine walked the long corridor to the school office to check for a message. Susan Farrell had said she would phone the school as soon as the results were known.

Eagle River was a tight-knit community. In calling around the night before to pass on the news about Seamus, Elaine had learned that a number of people—neighbors, state trooper friends of Jim's, nursing students friendly with Susan—were planning on dropping by the hospital to lend support. There would be sandwiches and snack food to nurse the Farrells through what everyone prayed would be a very long day.

The idea that the waiting room of Providence Medical Center might be the setting for something resembling a church social struck Elaine as very Alaska. Alaska is largely a land of transplants. Ravenwood families, and faculty as well, came from all across the United States. Teacher Peggy Kurzmann and her husband, Andy, had come here from central Michigan after college. Principal Arge Jeffery had migrated from Idaho seeking, in his words, "big fish." Joan Johnson was from Port Angeles, Washington. Fifth-grade teacher Dan Carey had been raised in Wisconsin. Audrey Chapman, another teacher, came from an island off the northern coast of Lake Michigan. Rachel Harrison, the other fourth-grade teacher, was from Spokane. Both PTA president Kay Pederson—whose son, AJ, was in Elaine's class—and her husband were from South Dakota. Barbara Bernard, another room parent, was an Alaskan, but her husband was from International Falls, Minnesota. Hardly anybody who lived here was from here.

Elaine herself was from rural Manitoba and had arrived in Alaska via Niles, Michigan, where she'd been a stay-at-home mom raising three daughters. Her husband, an impatient man with a yen for flying small planes, was employed as an air-traffic controller. Elaine had not even been aware that her husband was job hunting until one day he came home from work and said, "Guess what? We're moving to Alaska."

He had accepted a position—actively pursued it, Elaine was later to find out—at Anchorage's Merrill Field, one of the busiest light-plane airports in the world. In the year Elaine arrived, 1977, the state's economy was being transformed by the mammoth Trans-Alaska Pipeline that was being completed in order to transport newly discovered oil from Prudhoe Bay in the Arctic Ocean to the Lower 48. The word quickly spread. A boom was on!

Suddenly, Alaska was a mecca of full employment and soaring wages. To those who were predisposed to think of themselves as bold, individualistic, and, above all, eager for a brand-new start, Alaska was just the ticket. Seemingly overnight, commercial buildings, warehouses, apartments, roads, shopping centers, and subdivisions sprang up where there had been only wilderness. The population of Eagle River more than doubled in the space of a few years. There was a pressing need for more schools. And, of course, more teachers.

• • •

Eagle River is a town sandwiched between more than just mountain peaks. On the edge of a vast wilderness, it is home to several (maybe a few too many) late-twentieth-century strip malls. Men heading out to caribou hunts can stop for sustenance at KFC or Burger King or Taco Bell. Many residents hold vaguely antigovernment political views, yet with the nearby Elmendorf Air Force Base and the sprawling Army post at Fort Richardson, government service provides the direct or indirect livelihood for many in town and is an indispensable cornerstone of the regional economy. For every raunchy throwback of a saloon like Tips, there's a nail salon opening in a vacant storefront off Old Glenn Highway.

Eagle River, when Elaine arrived, had one foot in the old frontier, one kicking at the door of the new. During her first Christmas there, stuck in the dark valley knowing not a soul, she felt more isolated than she ever had in her life. But she knew what most people who live in the far north know, that neighbors and friends can become like family. Most of the people Elaine met were also first-generation residents. Like her, they were cut off by vast distance from relatives and extended family. They were not antisocial. In fact, the people she met in Alaska, with their eagerness to forge new friendships and fashion social networks to replace the ones they'd left behind, were as avid for fellowship as any she'd ever known.

The Farrells, too, were transplants. Jim had been raised in New Rochelle, New York. Growing up, he'd had two quite specific goals: he wanted to work in law enforcement, and he wanted to live as far as possible from traffic congestion. He'd first come to Alaska to visit a sister who was living on remote Kodiak Island. Instantly, he knew this was the place. He returned east to complete his schooling at Iona College with a degree in sociology, then promptly came back to Alaska to join the state troopers. With a thick moustache, square jaw, and rakish gleam in his dark eyes, he looked the part he was often called on to play, the lone lawman striding into a tough situation.

Susan was blonde, short, cute, and quick, with a natural singsong merriment in her voice. She had the type of sympathetic demeanor and upbeat outlook that make her anyone's perfect friend. She first met Jim when they were teenagers and they became friendly. Impetuously, she'd married another man. Shortly after her divorce, she was working at Benton & Bowles, the Manhattan advertising agency, when Jim, on one of his regular visits back east, looked her up. A few months later, they were married in Juneau, where Jim was stationed, by Judge Gerald Williams, a former trooper, at the home of one of Jim's fellow troopers. It was a full life, and not the least isolated or estranged. The Farrells enjoyed camping with their sons—nothing extreme, just car camping in spectacular settings—and fishing. They were not affluent, but were mostly free from major financial worries. Their world was largely peaceful and suburban, although there were reminders, often through Jim's work, that this land was still an unruly frontier and that trouble was out there somewhere.

Once, Jim had been called to a violent confrontation at a trailer park. He'd received a report that a man inside a trailer had chased a family out of it with a knife. It was midwinter and late, an hour of night and a time of year when alcohol consumption often played a role, and not a pretty one. Jim approached the trailer. He could hear loud music playing inside. He could also hear what sounded like a round being chambered into a rifle. Jim shouted to whoever was inside that he was a trooper. No response. He tried opening the door. It was locked. There was a small window on the upper part of the door and the man's face suddenly appeared in it. Jim ordered him to open up, and the man just smiled.

Over the years, Jim had lost enough fellow troopers to know that a drunken maniac in a midnight rage is exactly how the curtain can drop. Jim backed away. The man disappeared from the door. There was a brief lull. Jim cautiously approached the trailer once more, and peered into the window. The man was now seated on the couch. Jim watched him bend over, put the rifle to his chest, and shoot himself point-blank.

• • •

The Ravenwood holiday program was broken up into shifts due to space limitations. The afternoon program, which featured the younger grades, was a dress rehearsal for the evening program. The older kids, who'd made the sets and costumes and would perform in the evening, were in the audience in the afternoon (although the sixth graders were off campus at their skating party).

Elaine recognized that there was no point in attempting to have the class do too much during this interlude between lunch and their scheduled time onstage at the assembly. So she used the time to have them begin creating holiday cards to accompany the gifts the class would be giving to a needy family.

Each year Elaine contacted the Salvation Army in Anchorage and asked them to assign to her class a family in need, preferably one with at least one child who was approximately a fourth grader. The Salvation Army would provide a profile of the needy family and an outline of their modest "wish list" ("snow pants so I can play outside," "work clothes so Mom can get an office job").

Elaine asked each student to contribute five dollars to help buy gifts for this family. But there was a catch: they couldn't ask their parents for the money or go to their piggy banks. The money had to be earned. Each student had to describe the chores he or she did to earn the money: Shoveled neighbor's driveway. Stacked firewood. Cleaned out garage. They shared these details with each other at Circle Time while signing the card that went with the gift.

Elaine had put out plenty of supplies—colored construction paper, pens and crayons, glue and vials of glitter. The kids earnestly applied themselves to the card-making task.

One boy raised his hand. "Should we make a card for Seamus?"

Elaine hesitated. They had already written cards for Seamus.

"No," the boy said, as if he were reading her thoughts. "I mean, should we write our adopted family a card and say it's from him?"

"Yes," she answered. The kids really were learning. "That's an excellent idea."

The cards, which the kids were encouraged to embellish with decorations and fancy lettering, would go in a big sack along with many gifts, including a dollhouse and a kit for building model planes they'd purchased on a field trip into town.

When they were done with the cards, Elaine would tell her class, "You've given your time and effort to help someone in need. You've made our circle larger."

• • •

There was an enchanting timelessness about grammar school performances and productions. Elaine loved watching the youngsters determinedly going through their paces. She loved the earnest faces of the proud parents as they arched on tiptoes to get a clear camera angle for that perfect photo album snapshot. Events like the holiday program were, in some ways, the quintessence of childhood. The modest performances are like an embryonic cell, possessing a vast pluralism of potential. Someday one of these performers might turn into another . . . well, name your favorite: another Streep, or Hanks, or the strident singer with platinum hair currently topping the pop charts. That was the beauty of children, their boundless promise. You could imagine them becoming almost anything, and you would not be a fool for doing so.

Seeing all those parents clasping their hands, craning their necks, beaming like beacons, Elaine would silently urge them: Go ahead, go for it, imagine it all!

Yet there was another truth about school performances that invariably emerged when you've attended enough of them. They repeated themselves, season to season, year to year, and in the great wash of time, it did not really matter who stepped forward to play the lead or who cowered in the background sucking his thumb, who stumbled and who soared. Eventually each role—star as well as supporting cast—would get filled. All parts would eventually get performed. That's the way life was. Like the ceaseless cascade of a waterfall, you could step back from it, walk away, return after a moment or a day or a year to look again, and there it was! Still churning, still frothing, still flowing, still remarkably the same.

In the gym, all classes not currently taking their positions onstage were directed to sit on the floor in front. The back half of the gym was set up with folding chairs to accommodate parents and relatives. The place was a happy buzz. Late-arriving parents, some carting crying infants, scrambled to find seats.

Elaine's students filed in to their designated space on the gym floor and sat down. The third graders were first; then it would be their turn. Elaine watched from the entrance. Her kids knew what sort of behavior she expected of them, and today was no exception.

Principal Arge Jeffery stepped to the lip of the stage for his welcoming remarks. Then came the third graders, in elf caps and white shirts, squeaking out a shrill rendition of "Deck the Halls" on their plastic recorders. Elaine seized the opportunity to slip out and check again with the office. It was now almost two o'clock.

"Nothing yet," reported Melissa O'Guin, the school secretary, lifting her hand to show her crossed fingers.

Elaine allowed herself a guarded moment of hope. Although Susan Farrell had not gone into great detail except to outline the two main options—elaborate brain surgery or a hasty retreat—Elaine understood, or at least thought she did, that the surgeons would recoil from a third option. They would not undertake high-risk procedures that could leave Seamus in a diminished state.

Elaine returned to the gym. The fourth-grade contingent, which included her class and two others, would soon take the stage. They'd been rehearsing for weeks and were prepared, she hoped, to tackle a choreographed version of "Love in Any Language," that featured a special verse where they expressed the lyrics in sign language.

Christmas happens every year, Elaine thought to herself, ready or not. In Eagle River, it was always white with snow.

3

FIELD TRIP

As soon as Elaine walked into the hospital room, Seamus crowed, "Mrs. Moore! I've been waiting for you."

He was sitting up. His skull was wrapped in a thick bandage. An IV tube ran from the bedside apparatus to his arm. He was dressed in a pale blue hospital gown. Amazingly, he looked exactly the same. His voice was spunky. His eyes were bright. His obvious delight at her arrival mirrored what she'd seen nearly every morning when he arrived in Room 112.

He did not appear to be in pain. That was a blessing. Excitedly, Seamus showed Elaine the get-well cards tacked around his room, many from kids in the class. A friend of Susan's had brought them to the hospital that day so

Seamus could have them when he woke up from surgery. They were hand-made and decorated, perhaps a bit gaudily, with glued-on tinsel and colorful drawings. Each had a personal note.

Seamus asked if Elaine wanted to read the cards. "They're really neat," he told her.

Elaine told him she was going away to Australia for a couple weeks to see her daughter over the holiday break and that she looked forward to seeing Seamus as soon as she returned.

A nurse came in to say that Seamus really needed to rest. They said good-bye, and she was again astonished at how perky and like his old self he seemed. That had to be a good sign, she thought. Maybe the picture was not as bleak as the surface facts indicated.

The night before, after school, she'd learned the grim news. That tense yet promising afternoon interlude when Elaine had watched the clock with fingers crossed, believing each progressive hour, each *minute*, signaled an upgrade of Seamus's chances, had turned out to be a mirage. A delayed relay of information from the hospital, and not extensive surgery, had proved, sadly, to be the reality of what had taken place.

The surgeons operating on Seamus had discovered quite early that the tumor was massive and expanding rapidly. There was a brief consultation that served mostly to confirm the surgeons' preexisting conjecture. There was no way to extract the growth without severely damaging Seamus's brain. For all practical purposes, the tumor was inoperable. While sugarplum fairies were prancing across the Ravenwood stage, Seamus at Providence Medical Center had learned that his life would soon come to an end.

The doctors would put him on a radical regimen of radiation therapy. But the goal of those treatments would mainly be to retard the tumor's growth and provide a modicum of physical comfort during Seamus's remaining time on earth. There was nothing, in essence, to be done to alter the inevitable outcome.

Leaving Seamus's room, Elaine encountered Jim and Susan in the hospital corridor.

"You came!" they said. "Seamus said he knew you'd be coming."

Unlike Seamus, Susan and Jim looked haggard and grave. Elaine made a remark about how spirited Seamus seemed, and that's when Susan, her voice trembling, disclosed a detail Elaine had not yet heard.

"Six weeks," Susan said. "They told us he may have six weeks."

Elaine was stunned. Learning Seamus had an inoperable tumor had been shocking enough. But six weeks? Six weeks left to his life? That was a blink. A twitch. That was nothing. It was almost like having no time at all.

A radical wild card, Elaine suddenly realized, had been introduced. It was too soon to know exactly what she would do or exactly how she would respond. But it was not too soon to recognize that something had happened to the community of Room 112. They would of course go on. But they would not go on as if nothing had happened. This school year—at least what remained of it—was going to be very different. It was not going to unfold as planned.

• • •

One of the marvels of teaching for Elaine was the kaleido-scopic range of possibilities that existed for any one class. Before the start of the school year, she was presented with a list—your basic computer printout of students—and she might be tempted to make some vague conjectures about what dynamics would result. She would have some basic information, some advance "intelligence," drawn from school records, remarks from other teachers, experience with older siblings, plus stray observations made at the playground or cafeteria. But that only gave her a limited glimpse of individual children based on their performances in the past. It told nothing, or very close to nothing, about the consideration that most consumed her: how would the children come together as a group?

Each class was unique. Each held surprises. Each had its own collective personality and an evolving one, different in early September than it was come May. It was this group quality, this sense of who they were as a collection of individ-uals whose full identity would be realized only in close associ-ation with each other, that Elaine was most keen to cultivate.

Some classes were more passive than she might like.

Others took her injunction to be social in their learning a bit too far, and had to be reined in. Classes had temperaments, both dominant and recessive, and the temperaments could shift without warning. Controlling their every antic, she had come to realize, was not a battle worth waging. Shaping them, directing them, cultivating them? That was more like it. She very much saw her function as "guide on the side," as the phrase goes.

One year Elaine's students got the idea to raise money through a skate-a-thon in order to help a local family whose house had been damaged by fire. Another class collected books to distribute at an Anchorage homeless shelter. Another gathered clothing to send to children in Bangladesh.

This year's class had quickly blasted off to an impressive start. Below Ravenwood, on the hillside slanting toward Eagle River, was a modest outdoor amphitheater that was sometimes used by classes for outdoor lessons. Over the summer, it had been vandalized. Log seats had been over-turned and damaged. Some had been chopped up and burned. Garbage had been strewn about, and the turf had been badly gouged. Elaine's students, like the rest of the school, learned of this only when they returned to school in September.

Immediately they began discussing—and researching—ways to repair the amphitheater. There'd been an announce-ment that a community schools program was offering a grant worth $250 for a project that would benefit all students, and application forms would be available in the school office. With scant prodding from Elaine, the kids fetched an application and submitted it. They needed the grant, they wrote, primarily for building materials, such as pressurized, weather-treated wood. Against the odds, they were awarded the grant. This class was off and running!

In October, Elaine shared an article with the class (she periodically brought in news items to discuss at Circle Time) that reported on books that were being banned in some communities. Books were powerful things, she explained, so powerful that sometimes they were banned by people who were actually afraid of the ideas contained in them, or, as was often the case, the ideas they *thought* were contained in them.

Well, the kids found this outrageous, especially upon learning that Dr. Seuss, their beloved Dr. Seuss, was one of the targets of those protests. His whimsical environmentalist fable, *The Lorax*, was on several lists of targeted books.

One boy, the precocious Hans Bernard, declared that something should be done.

"Why not?" Elaine responded with enthusiasm, telling the kids they might be onto something.

They formed a committee. They held meetings at recess time. They made placards. They made a poster comprised of illustrated squares, each one depicting a book that was banned or challenged. They wrote a letter to the local newspaper.

"We have a concern," the letter began. "People are trying

to ban books for unfair reasons. So many of our favorite books are being banned. Classics like *Little Red Riding Hood* and *Alice in Wonderland* are being banned. In *Little Red Riding Hood*, the wolf eats the grandma. We see things a lot worse on TV every day. I am glad to live in a ban-free state. Let's keep it that way."

The *Chugiak–Eagle River Star* ran a piece about the kids' activities, accompanied by a photo of proud Hans and seven beaming classmates hoisting placards: CELEBRATE FREEDOM— READ A BANNED BOOK and IT'S A BOOK—WHY NOT READ IT?

Of course, such achievements were not necessarily monumental in the grand scheme of things. A restored outdoor amphitheater was not the Taj Mahal. The *Chugiak–Eagle River Star* was not the *New York Times*. But Elaine Moore worked on a smaller canvas. Learning— the real stuff—was bursting out all over. The genie was out of the bottle, and in her experience, it generally never went back in.

So she never knew how a class would develop. The start of each school year was like the beginning of a river rafting trip. She knew little about the water ahead except the general direction of it (flowing past the necessary curriculum checkpoints) and where it eventually emptied out (early June, and matriculation to the next grade level). The river could get rough. There could be interludes of tranquility. But there would always, *always* be surprises.

Each year was an improvisation within the constraints of preestablished forms. Collaborative jazz was a better metaphor for Elaine's approach than the precision of classical music. But there was a constant: every season she would make a point of announcing to the children, right at the outset, what she believed was the fundamental, overarching truth about this enterprise we call school.

"This year," she would tell them, "we are going to learn to love learning. That is our main goal. Always keep that in mind. Learning is what life's about. We are going to be learners not just this year, not just while we're in school. We will be learners throughout our lives. We will be learning until the day we die. In fact, if we stop learning, we call that dying."

• • •

The twenty-three-hour flight to see her daughter Leigh Anne in Australia left Elaine with plenty of time for reflection.

Seamus's situation was nearly impossible to accept. "Terminal" was the phrase the doctors had apparently used, a word that carried within it the cold steel slam of a windowless prison door. Elaine's immediate thoughts were for Seamus. What kind of pain would he suffer? How rapidly would he deteriorate? And what of his ebullient spirit? How does a person, much less a child, come to terms with a prognosis so bleak, so final, so manifestly unfair?

Her thoughts were also with Seamus's family. Susan and Jim had impressed her as such good people. "Good," of course, was a vastly overused term, especially around schools, but in some ways you could not find a more apt phrase for the Farrells. They exuded it in all its qualities, both overt and subtle. They cared about others. They were interested in others. They asked how *you* were doing even when they were phoning to say their son was dying! How would they cope?, Elaine wondered. How would they control the rampage of their own emotions while at the same time caring for and consoling Seamus?

Finally, there was her class, the twenty-five other fourth graders she'd worked so hard to mold into a cohesive circle. It had been such a wonderful year so far, so productive, so exemplary, so promising. What, she wondered, was she going to do with the class now? What to tell them? How to tell them? This school year had been flowing so beautifully; what would become of it now?

There was an image of Seamus that Elaine couldn't get out of her head. It was from early in the fall. He'd been walking close behind her, almost too close, and he seemed eager to tell her something. Other children were bunching up to her heels and she had to tell Seamus to wait, she'd get to his question in a minute. Waiting a minute when he was bursting with something to say was not Seamus Farrell's strongest attribute. She'd had to laugh. He looked like he would explode with impatience.

The class had been on a field trip to the Eagle River Nature Center, a gorgeous stretch of winding wilderness trails surrounded by glacial peaks. They were hiking in an area that crossed the famed Iditarod Trail (an early section of the original dogsled route over Crow Pass). It was the first week of school, right after Labor Day.

Elaine insisted on, *believed in*, taking her class on field trips at the very outset of the school year. Principal Jeffery referred to her as the Field Trip Queen, a bit disparagingly, she always thought—as though she were trying to get out of "real" teaching! Other teachers were astonished that she would attempt a daylong outing so soon after the start of school.

"What if someone gets lost?" one colleague warned. "You don't even know their names yet."

"It's worth the risk," Elaine joked.

By that, she meant that the rewards of seeing how the kids behaved outside the school environment were substantial, and the earlier she could observe them, and interact with them in a nonacademic setting, the better. A field trip was the perfect way for her to learn about the children and for them to learn about her.

Besides, early September was when the salmon were spawning and that was something she wanted the class to experience together. It happened at no other time in the year. It was now or never. Fur trappers, she liked to point out, might wish for milder temperatures in which to go about trapping animals, but it was in the bitter cold of midwinter that animal pelts were fullest. She wanted them to understand that you had to adapt to nature. That was the point of it.

A walk through the woods and a picnic by the river could

reveal characteristics about each child, and the class as a whole, that could take her months to learn in the confines of a schoolroom. Who pushed into the lead? Who were the followers? Who clumped together and socialized with whom? Which ones were reluctant to guess at answers? Which were nimble on their feet? Which children kept to themselves? Which possessed a keenness and intuition about nature?

Over the years, Elaine had noticed that kids who did not especially shine in the classroom, who were clumsy or inattentive when it came to standard academic work, who might even be construed as slow learners, often churned with inquisitiveness and brimmed with insights amid an old-growth forest or an estuary teeming with marine life. If she had kids like that in her class, she wanted to know it as early in the school year as possible.

Of course the field trip was not all about what their teacher needed to learn about *them*. She had prepped them with briefings concerning aspects of the woods and river valley to observe, plus questions they should try to answer. Why are some rocks rounded, why are they smooth? Why does fungi grow where it does? Why not on your shoes? There would be a lichen lesson, a mushroom lesson, a tree-bark lesson, and more.

"You might think you are fourth graders," she told them, "but really you are naturalists."

"What's a naturalist?" someone would ask.

"Someone who studies and appreciates nature," she

would answer. "And the only tools that a naturalist needs are a notebook (which you have), a pencil (which you have), and your senses."

"That's all?"

"Yes. You're all naturalists."

• • •

At the nature center, the launching point for their hike, the kids were greeted by a small poster board on which the daily "Bear Alert" was announced. Here were posted any sightings of grizzlies or black bears over the past several days. A wooden sign at the start of the trail warned, BEARS PRESENT IN AREA/TAKE PROPER PRECAUTIONS.

Elaine liked to have the entire class pose for a photograph directly in front of this sign. "So your parents will at least have one last picture of you." She said this with a hint of a smile, letting the ones who were not yet on to her know that she was probably joking.

The common wisdom about bears in the Alaska woods is that they are dangerous only if they are surprised. Making noise while hiking is considered the best preventive. In that regard, a collection of twenty-five fourth graders fresh from summer vacation, showing off for each other and for their new teacher, chattering and laughing, created something very close to bear immunity. At least along this much-visited stretch of the valley.

Elaine asked the children to walk behind her. That was

one of the rules of the outing; nobody could pass her. They could bunch up as close to her heels as they wished, but they were not allowed to pass. To make sure she got to know each child a little over the course of the hike, Elaine would invite different students to share the lead with her. At this early stage of the school year, it was not thought a punishment to be summoned forward by the teacher.

They proceeded along the Albert Loop Trail as it sliced through meadow and forest toward the river. They passed a thicket of bright yellow devil's club shimmering in the high September sun. She asked the children to identify this plant based on data sheets that were part of their packet.

"Look at its stems," she'd coax.

"Wow! Those things are like daggers."

"And its height."

"Taller than me!"

She explained that Native American peoples would mash this plant into salves or let it seep into tea as a remedy for ailments ranging from ulcers to tuberculosis.

"People used to use plants like this as their medicine cabinet," she explained.

It wasn't just certain types of children who came into their own outdoors. Elaine did, too. Here in the woods, alertly shifting her gaze from tree stumps to treetops, hiking with the self-assurance of a forest creature in its natural habitat, deftly leading the kids like a wilderness guide, it was sometimes hard for her to believe she had come so far.

• • •

Elaine was raised in the prairie town of Douglas, Manitoba, one hundred miles west of Winnipeg, the middle of five children of subsistence farmers who espoused old-world values of hard work, diligence, and thrift. It was a rustic upbringing that had more in common with the nineteenth century than the twentieth.

Her grade-school education took place entirely in a one-room schoolhouse. Eight grades—thirty or more sons and daughters of local farm families—bunched together in one room for the entire school day. Desks were bolted to the floorboards in straight rows. The teacher stood in front, daring any child to challenge her authority.

Strangely, it was a smoothly functioning environment, and not simply because of the stern discipline imposed by an authoritarian teacher. Rather, it was cooperative. Older children who'd finished their assignments helped out the younger ones. Faster learners willingly tutored slower learners. What is now known as "peer tutoring"—but was not then identified as such—was an indispensable tool. For the teacher could not possibly have enough time to tend to all the varied needs of such a wide range of students.

Elaine was a model student by the modest standards of her farm community. She was a classic do-gooder, always anxious to please. As early as in first grade, she found herself called upon to assist other students who were struggling, even kids several years older. She found she was adept at taking the little painted wooden pegs used for demonstrating basic math concepts and showing faltering students how it worked: you combine three groups consisting of four pegs each and—voilà!—multiplication!

She liked doing it, liked breaking down what she knew into component parts in order to explain it to another. She liked seeing the satisfaction in the eyes of a student who went from incomprehension to comprehension. It was such a neat feeling, combining the pleasure of solving a puzzle with the pleasure of helping someone. Talk about multiplication!

After she'd finished work at her desk and had no other tasks to attend to, Elaine would daydream. What would it be like, she wondered, to be the teacher? Many children have powerful visions of what they want to be when they grow up. These range from the fanciful (pro baseball player) to the semipreposterous (poet) to the reasonably achievable (nurse). Elaine Moore knew: she wanted to grow up to be a teacher.

Like an apprentice in training, Elaine keenly observed the methods and tactics of her teacher. And she took careful note of what *not* to do, too. Mrs. Peterson had a particularly jarring way of handling kids who weren't keeping up. When a child was called upon to answer aloud in front of the room and responded in a way that Mrs. Peterson found lacking, she would demonstrate her displeasure by ceremonially aiming her forefinger directly at her own temple and making the loudest noise she could—"Pow!"—to imitate the sharp report of a discharged gun at close range.

It got the kids' attention. And Elaine's. She made a mental note *never* to do that when she became a teacher.

In the one-room schoolhouse in Douglas, all children, grades one through eight, sat down to lunch together. At recess, older kids often needed the youngsters to fill out teams for a game, be it kickball or your basic snowball fight. Not until Elaine was well into her own teaching career was she able to look back at the little schoolhouse in Douglas and fully appreciate it for what it was: a true community.

• • •

"Stop," Elaine suddenly instructed her students.

Word shot backward through the group: "Teacher says stop."

"What do you smell?" Elaine asked.

"Fresh air," someone shouted.

Elaine had to smile. For now, she would accept "fresh air" as a suitable answer. She wanted to get the kids used to using their senses—*all* of them. She wanted to instill a vigilance toward the incredible world that surrounded them. There was a little game she'd developed to foster their observational skills as they walked along the forest path. Every time they saw or heard or smelled or sensed something interesting, they were to whisper (never shout), "Spot it!" and thereby bring the object to the attention of their classmates.

It took a while, but a half an hour into their hike, "Spot

it!" was starting to ring out with increasing frequency. A toadstool nestled in ferns. Lichen atop a fallen limb.

"Spot it!"

Beaver-teeth markings on a dead tree stump.

"Spot it!"

A cavelike hollow in the base of a huge tree, just the right size to make a home for the Berenstain Bears.

"Spot it!"

"You're nature detectives," Elaine told them. "You need to be on the lookout for clues."

Here was a cottonwood tree. How do you know it? By the type of crevasses in the bark and the alignment of veins on its leaves.

They passed a patch of horsetail. This plant was identifiable by its tall, upright stems that looked a bit like asparagus stalks branching out to resemble horse's tails.

"This is an interesting plant," she said. "You should take a picture of it."

"Mrs. Moore," one girl complained. "I don't have a camera."

Elaine showed them what she meant. She framed the image by squaring her thumb and forefinger in front of her squinting eye, and then said, "Click." "You don't need a camera," she pointed out. "You can take a picture with your mind."

Instantly, they all began swiveling to find suitable snapshots—with their minds. Click. Click. Click.

The horsetail plant, she explained, was among the oldest

and most hardy species around. They first appeared some 400 million years ago and were in the second group of plants ever to appear on earth. They dated from the Jurassic and Triassic periods, and once shared the land with the dinosaurs.

"Like a brontosaurus?" someone asked.

"Yes," she replied.

"A tyrannosaurus could have touched this?" another child asked, running his hand over the tail.

"Well, not this exact plant." In sparking their curiosity, you still had to respect the facts. "But one like it."

The trail periodically featured interpretive signs highlighting noteworthy natural features or, for the curious, directing attention to ecological concepts that were ripe for discussion. They passed a sign that read, CAN A SNOWFLAKE CARVE A VALLEY?

Elaine waited for the class to bunch around her. She read the question aloud. "Can a snowflake carve . . . ?"

"Yes!" they shouted in near-unison.

"Really? This magnificent valley could have been carved by snowflakes?"

"Yes!"

The relationship between snowfall and melt, the fusing of ice crystals into glacial ice, and the gradual sculpting of landscape over the course of thousands of years was a primary lesson. The spot they now stood on, Elaine said, was once a river of ice. She had them gaze (she preferred that they gawk) at the six-thousand-foot peaks immediately surrounding them (Eagle Peak is 6,955 feet high) and imagine what this valley would have been like thousands of years ago when it was filled solid, all the way to the mountain peaks, with ice.

"Wow!"

Yes, she thought. That was exactly the right response. Wow, indeed!

They passed a thick grove of tall cottonwood and spruce trees. The path was dirt and pebble. The sweet fall air was filled with the rhythmic pattering of size-five sneakers on soft ground. Wind rushed through the high leaves above.

"Stop," Elaine instructed them. "Listen."

The children hushed. Sunlight filtering through the high trees seemed to dance on the dirt of their path. There was another sound, the groan and creak of lumber against its grain. They were approaching the river and the grove of nearby quaking aspen.

"What do you hear?" she asked.

At first, nobody answered. She wanted them to know that she valued children who noticed things, and she didn't mind if they became a bit competitive for her approval. She cupped her hand to her ear. She waited.

"The river."

Yes, they were close enough to hear its constant, peaceful churn.

"Wood," someone answered.

"It's whining," another said.

There was some chuckling. But Elaine liked this answer

and she let them know by asking who'd said it. No one immediately stepped forward to own up to it. She looked them over.

They were a handsome, scrubbed, middle-class group, a little scruffy, with the usual runny noses and mildly unkempt hair and clothes that had probably been a perfect fit for the older sibling who'd outgrown them. It was true, she did not know all their names perfectly just yet. At least not without a moment's thought.

There was Hans Bernard, Elizabeth Williams, Erick Clouse, Lauren Smith, Danielle Whitehead, Arriane Bicher, Logan Tucker, Frank Weiss, Sarah Ann Chapman, Melody Kalowski, Alexandra Vanderhoff, Sarah Cobb, Paul Hackenmueller, Michelle Foss, Jacob Simpson, Rebecca Olson, Michelle Moore (no relation to Elaine), Cullen Kurzmann, Austin (AJ) Pederson, David Schwartz, Dylan McDonald, Daniel Lee, Laura Peters, James Lockwood, and Seamus Farrell.

It was a large class. But she'd had large classes in the past. There were ways to manage them. And it was all the more reason to encourage them to look out for each other.

It was nearing lunchtime. They would picnic by the salmon-spawning area. The stream at this point on the Albert Loop Trail was a shallow tributary to the Eagle River and provided a great place to observe the salmon as they engaged in their primordial struggle to reproduce. As predictable as the post–Labor Day start of the school year was the fall spawning of the sockeye and coho salmon.

The salmon occupies a position of symbolic as well as real importance in Alaskan culture. The marvelous silver fish with its famously indomitable will represents, subtly or overtly, a point of pride with Alaskans. It would not be an exaggeration to say that most Alaskans have some direct involvement with the fish, if only peripherally—or know someone who does.

A huge commercial industry is dependent on salmon, generating more than $200 million per year and employing as many as twenty thousand people in various capacities, including fishermen, boat operators, processors, exporters, brokers, and more. In addition, there are numerous Alaskans who, like Napa Valley property owners awakening to the pleasure and profit in growing luscious grapes as a side income, engage in commercial salmon fishing on a non-industrial, second-income scale, acquiring rights from the government to string nets across designated sections of rivers and making arrangements with restaurants and distributors to deliver their catch. Rachel Harrison, another fourth-grade teacher at Ravenwood, and her husband, a computer-systems specialist with the state of Alaska, did precisely this on a stretch of the Ivan River up by Willow, thirty miles north of Eagle River.

Sport fishing for salmon abounds, and not just for the resident Alaskans. Tourists come to fish, and the state's tourism industry is avid to capitalize on the activity of salmon fishing. "Super Affordable Clear Stream Alaska Salmon Fishing," one lodge advertises. "Imagine yourself in

Alaska, far from civilization, standing in a clear river, loaded with trophy salmon and arctic char just 100 yards from your private Alaska fishing lodge, pristine wilderness as far as the eye can see, and no one else around."

But there is more than commerce or recreation behind the Alaskan affinity for salmon. There are qualities about the fish itself, and its seemingly heroic fight for survival against immense odds, that are central to its place of endearment in Alaskan hearts and minds.

Elaine loved to regale her kids with fish facts: Some salmon travel two thousand miles over a period of up to two months to arrive at their spawning ground, and they accomplish all this without eating *any* food! To surmount waterfalls that block their path upstream, salmon sometimes leap twelve feet or higher. Salmon are able to navigate homeward through unbelievably complicated waters, both ocean and river, steering partly by means of a unique sense of smell. For example, scientists have demonstrated that salmon can detect one drop of water from its home stream mixed into 250 gallons of seawater. They are fish, above all else, that know where home is, have extraordinary tools for finding it, and will stop at nothing to get there. Talk about motivated!

Elaine led the class to the wooden platform overlooking the spawning area. This was an ideal spot for lunch. There were built-in benches for some of the kids to sit on. For those who wanted to continue their observations, there were plenty of weary, emaciated salmon on the last leg of their heroic odyssey flopping and floundering in the clear shallow waters right beneath the wooden bridge.

Some children plunked down and went straight for the peanut butter sandwiches and bags of chips. Others approached the guardrail hanging over the river.

The children had read together an interpretive sign titled A LIFETIME OF CHANGE that detailed the salmon cycle. But there was nothing like witnessing the real thing. There was a timeless ritual occurring down there, on clear view just a few yards away. Elaine took note of which children were drawn to it. Boys, it seemed, found this most fascinating. Without comprehending the specific concept of "dominant male" and its function in salmon reproduction or, for that matter, the survival of the species, many of Elaine's boys— and some of the girls—detected a decidedly combatlike competitiveness in the desperate thrashing taking place in the water just a few feet below.

"Look at that guy!" one boy squealed, pointing to a bright red fish with its distinctive deep green head (the tell-tale sign that its life is nearing its end), vigorously nipping at several others, nudging them away.

"Yeah, that guy's tough."

"Look at that one. He's tougher."

"Oh yeah?"

"That guy's the toughest."

The female salmon with its dark red body and green head and tail had dug her nest, or *redd*, in a bed of stones in clear shallow water directly beneath the wooden platform. The redd is an indentation in the riverbed where the female deposits her eggs. Commonly, the female digs several redds, and this is done by beating her tail against the bottom, sweeping stones away and hollowing out a depression somewhat larger than her body. While digging out her redd, the female is often accompanied by several males who will then compete for the opportunity to court her before depositing their sperm.

Fifth grade was where sex ed—or "Human Growth and Development," as it was called—became a featured (and much-discussed) supplement to the curriculum. Salmon reproduction, Elaine figured, was an acceptable primer that avoided, thank you, any hot-button concepts and roughly coincided with what most of the kids already knew. Sperm and egg and two fish lying side by side in a nest sculpted from the pebbled floor of a glacier-fed stream, with the September sun warming the day and glinting off glacial peaks framed by the vivid blue sky—well, that is how life continues on our planet.

After twenty minutes for lunch, Elaine gathered the children together for another lesson related to salmon. This was sort of a math lesson—math edging into mystery. She pointed to a few of the slowly disintegrating salmon, listing and sinking and floating to the surface, each a pale—literally—shadow of its former self. "See these," Elaine pointed. "Five years ago, they hatched right here, all by themselves, without a mother or father around. They grew up in this river and after a while they migrated out to the Pacific Ocean and spent a few years there and now—can you imagine?—they have come all the way back to the very spot where they were hatched. And this is where they will die."

It might have seemed odd for Elaine to speak of dying in tones that were so upbeat and even admiring. But nature was like that, she believed. There was a marvel to every occurrence.

And then the numbers. The kids were not very far along in their understanding of mathematics, but these numbers, she was sure, they could grasp. This was the sort of lesson she loved and she went at it with special enthusiasm. Each of these female salmon, she told the kids, will produce some four thousand eggs. From these four thousand eggs, some four hundred fry (babies) emerge. Of these four hundred fry, some forty will survive and develop into smolt, the adult salmon that become a bright silver in the sea. Depending on the species, the adult will live some one to five years in the ocean. From those forty smolt, only four will survive to make the arduous journey back to the stream where they were born. Of those four returning smolt, two will go on to spawn. And spawning, this weary spasm of a death dance that the kids were leaning over the railing to observe, is the crowning jewel of the adventurous existence of an Alaskan salmon. For it leads to the only consensus definition of success for living things who lack the hubris of mankind: namely, passing on one's genes to a next generation. The odds against success—if dodging myriad treacheries for the singular purpose of returning to the same tranquil valley where one was hatched can be said to define success—are staggering.

"What about all the other salmon?" Elaine asked the kids. "All those salmon that never made it back here? What happened to them?"

"They got eaten," one child offered.

"Caught by fishermen."

"Bears," someone suggested.

"All good answers," Elaine noted, and she proceeded to list the many creatures that are sustained by consuming salmon in one or more states of their development: black and brown bear; birds, including kingfishers and eagles and ducks; larger fish like sharks; sea mammals such as whales and dolphins, and, of course, human beings, from Native American tribes on the Kenai Peninsula to diners at expensive restaurants in midtown Manhattan.

"Nothing ever truly dies in nature," Elaine pointed out with a lift in her voice to let them know that this part was really important. "All these creatures are *supported* by the salmon who are born here but never make it back."

"Support" was the operative word. Elaine preferred not to call the salmon "prey" for these other species. It wasn't that she wanted to sugarcoat the reality of what happened in nature. Rather, she felt they should appreciate the big picture: the ongoing, intricately woven, perpetually replenishing relationships between living things on this earth. Yes, there was the fact of dog-eat-dog and the grueling survival of the fittest. But the overriding reality was that life was inarguably, overwhelmingly, a cycle. The fallen tree starting to decay was food for teeming larvae that would become some larger creature's sustenance. In the end, when you stepped back in humble admiration of the great miracle of nature, what you saw was the timeless, seamless flow, a beginning making its way inexorably to an ending that then launched a new beginning.

Elaine recalled looking the class over and liking what she'd seen so far. They did not appear overly clique-ish. Not too much teasing. There was interaction between boys and girls. A few of the kids who were not reputed to be the strongest students had, true to form, led the way with numerous "Spot-its."

"What," she decided to ask them, "do we humans support?"

How humans come to occupy segments in the food chain was not precisely the answer she was after, at least not explicitly. In truth, she had no particular answer in mind. It was an open-ended, provocative question, with multiple implications, not all of them ecological. She wanted to see where the children might go with this.

Hans Bernard raised his hand. His mother had been a teacher. He had been raised to be thoughtful and ethical, in addition to which he had a knack for argument. "Do we support the environment," Hans asked, with the clear implication that he knew the answer, "or do we just take from it?"

Elaine smiled. This was certainly going to be an interesting class. She loved this grade, this age.

There was something special, Elaine believed, that coalesced in children around the age of ten—their cognitive ability was enhanced, their social skills were expanding, yet they retained all the innocence and curiosity of pure childhood. The shadows of adolescence might be starting to gather, but its complications were still far enough away to be ignored. It was the age, roughly, of Peter Pan. Great adventures were to be had just by being together.

Several times during the day, Elaine had the students take a seat, on a log or a rock or the ground, open their notebooks to a blank page, and do a three-minute—she lifted the wrist with her watch on it to emphasize that this would be timed—fast write.

"About something you've seen or heard or smelled or thought today," she explained. She wanted them to master the habit of noticing and recording their observations, like a naturalist would. Later, back in class, she would have them refer to these notes in order to write a poem or story or essay.

"But what if . . ."

"Ready," she said. "Go."

The kids looked around, at the glacier looming above the valley, at the birds flitting between tall branches, at the pebbles along the path, at each other, checking out who was already busily writing.

Seamus, employing his notes from that day, later wrote:

"Salmon spawning/ Squirrels eating/ Ripe berries/ Crusty lichen/ Happy is how I felt."

• • •

Then it came to Elaine, relaxing in her seat en route to Australia—the missing detail she had tried to recall about that early September outing to the Chugach State Park.

They'd been hiking in the woods. There was a point where the path looped about and split and it was not obvious which fork was the correct choice. The morning was beautiful. The air was mild and dry. The woods were fragrant with moist earth and fallen leaves. Elaine paused, feigning deep puzzlement (she really wasn't *that* puzzled, but the kids didn't know that), and said in her soft, clear voice, "Oh, my. Are we lost?"

It was Seamus who'd pushed up beside her, asserting himself among the other kids. He eagerly pointed. "That way, Mrs. Moore!" To the right. That was the way to go. He was sure of it. And he was so proud, as kids always were, to be able to help in a pinch.

"Seamus, thank goodness you're with us," Elaine recalled remarking with a bit of exaggeration to let him know how much she valued his input. "We might be lost without you."

· 4 ·

TERMINAL

Cancer, illness, and the specter of death were not matters that were foreign to Elaine. Nor was the task of dealing with children concerning issues so gloomy and dire. Two years earlier, she herself had been stricken with breast cancer.

It had come as a shock, as it usually does. Elaine at that time was forty-eight years old and in excellent health. As a girl, she'd been a classic tomboy. She'd ridden horses and tended cattle, and was comfortable with the grit of the outdoors. She was an eager ballplayer and skater. She'd played hockey goalie using thick magazines banded around her thin legs for padding while her brothers and other boys swatted pucks at her across the frozen pond. Whenever she mentioned this to her students, they invariably responded in astonishment, "You played hockey, Mrs. Moore?"

Had she been raised in a Title 9 era more sympathetic to women's sports, she would have made a serious pursuit of competitive athletics. On moving to Alaska, she became an avid hiker and skier, both cross-country and downhill. She coached sports teams at the schools where she taught, boys' as well as girls', and seized every opportunity to play in the various student–faculty baseball or basketball contests that schools often featured as a year-end celebration or fundraiser.

Her cancer diagnosis was a blow. The particular sensitivities surrounding breast cancer added an additional layer of social awkwardness. Elaine had a hard time telling people about it, and a hard time making the sudden transition from absolute faith in her body's fortitude to serious doubts about her life expectancy. She had a hard time adapting her generous concern for the well-being of others to the more pressing concern of what was wrong with her and what needed to be done to set it right. But she knew without hesitation that she needed to tell her students.

Her diagnosis had come the day before spring break. After an intense period of reading up on all her options and seeking additional medical opinions, she'd opted for bilateral surgery—a double mastectomy—which took place in March. Immediately afterward, she began a six-month regime of chemotherapy. Doctors advised her to take the remainder of the school year off to recuperate. Elaine, however, found she was not as debilitated by the treatments as the doctors had predicted. Furthermore, she missed her class. "I needed those twenty-nine little distractions," she explained.

When she returned to teaching, less than two weeks following her surgery, she asked the children to circle up. The kids obviously knew something was wrong with her. She'd been absent from class and it was known that she'd been in the hospital. Children were bound to have heard bits and pieces of information, or rumors passing as information.

Some people had advised her not to tell the kids. The topic was too touchy, too grim, too emotionally charged, too far beyond their comprehension.

Elaine sat down with them at Circle Time. She reminded herself to sound as normal as possible. She wanted to inform them, but not alarm them. Instantly, she was struck by how different the dynamic was with children in comparison to adults. As her colleague Joan observed, "Kids come at you with love. They don't come at you with pity."

In her soft, reassuring voice she told them in clear, straightforward terms that she had cancer. There was a tumor in her breast, and she'd had it surgically removed. She explained to them that cancer was uncontrolled growth of abnormal cells and that its causes were largely mysterious. She told them what cancer was, and what it was not. It was not, for example, contagious. She explained that surgery was usually the preferred treatment, with radiation and chemotherapy also widely used. She told the children what each procedure entailed, and tried to do so in a way that was factual and informative and that conveyed her own optimism that the treatments would be successful.

Then she awaited their response. Would they be shocked? Upset? Worried?

There was audible relief. Some children began to smile. She knew their faces in all their expressive modes. These were smiles not of mirth or pleasure, but of relief.

"Oh, is that all?" one boy said.

For an instant, Elaine assumed he had misunderstood her.

"I knew it was in your chest," another boy said. "And I know you don't smoke so I didn't think it was your lungs."

"My grandfather had cancer," a girl chimed in.

Elaine waited for the depressing continuation of this account. But that was all the girl wanted to say.

"So'd mine," a boy added.

"We thought it was something a lot worse," another boy said.

"Like your heart or something."

"Or your stomach."

The children were just plain relieved. That—not horror, not fright, not pity—was their primary response. *Cancer* was a term they knew. It was concrete. It was real. It was, Elaine came to understand, far less frightening to the kids than the vast hole of being kept in the dark.

This confirmed her longstanding supposition that children can handle the truth, even hard truths; what they can't handle is not knowing.

"You can ask me any question you have about this," Elaine told them. "Now, or any other time you want."

"Will you die from this?"

Elaine did not flinch. "I could. But I intend to fight this illness. And I hope to live for a very long time."

They seemed to like that answer, and so did she.

• • •

Seamus spent several days recuperating from surgery at Providence. A group of active-duty marines, affiliated with the Toys for Tots program, came by with presents to cheer him up. They told Seamus what a tough little kid he was and how impressed they were to know a boy who was determined to defeat this disease, just as a Marine would do.

A little girl of toddler size carrying a giant white stuffed bear nearly as big as herself stopped into Seamus's room in the pediatric surgery ward and left the bear beside his bed while he was dozing. She told a nurse that she "wanted to give it to a sick child." Seamus awakened and found the bear, but he wanted to know who the girl was and why she'd been so nice to him. Jim and Susan went along the corridors asking doctors, nurses, staff, and patients in nearby rooms. Nobody knew. The girl had come and quietly delivered the bear and vanished. It was like a scene from a children's book or, depending on the reading level, the entirety of a children's book.

How would the book develop? Why was the girl at the

hospital? Was she visiting someone in trouble—her mother or father or sister?—or was she the one afflicted with a serious illness? Would the girl turn out to be an angel? Or, as Seamus might prefer, a benevolent alien? Would the incrementally complex quest to locate her transport the Farrells into magical realms? Would they travel through tunnels and over bridges and across mountains until they finally arrived at a tranquil oasis where they would discover it all to be just a dream—the little girl, the giant stuffed bear, *and* the tumor?

So many of life's events can be seen as parts of a story . . . if you are only able to relax and consider them with a little detachment.

Another day, the reigning Miss Alaska, Keri Baumgardner (who'd previously held the title of Miss Cook Inlet), stopped by the pediatric ward on a goodwill tour. She visited Seamus's room and gave him a big wet kiss on his blushing cheek, which embarrassed him probably because he enjoyed it so much. For a young boy, Seamus had a considerable eye for girls. It was a precocious quality, the kind that might cause his parents—and the parents of the girls— to worry a few years down the road.

Seamus's three brothers were present for much of the time he was in the hospital. They were important figures in his life. Jesse was a sixth grader at Ravenwood, a rough-and-tumble boy with muscles already in evidence. Joseph Adami, the child of Susan's first marriage back in New York, was ten years older than Seamus. He was a student at the

University of Alaska–Anchorage, and lived in a dormitory just a short walk from the hospital.

The third brother was Seamus's identical twin, Colin. An identical-twin relationship is more intense, more complex, more intimate than almost any other. Seamus's relationship with Colin was, if possible, even deeper than that.

Colin had the same crazy, cowlick-whorled hair, the same lithe build, the same elfin pucker at the corners of his mouth. But nearly everything else about Colin was different. The dazzling twinkle that was ever-present in Seamus's bright blue eyes was harder to detect in his twin brother's. Where Seamus's face seemed always on the verge of mirth, Colin seemed beset by inner struggle. The simple boyish pursuits that brought so much pleasure to Seamus, from ball sports to reading to exploring the woods, brought frustration to Colin or were simply beyond his capabilities. Where Seamus was most comfortable in the scruff and mess of dirt and mud and snow, Colin had a tactile aversion to them bordering on phobia. The very same wonderful world that was Seamus's perpetual playground often amounted to his twin's quicksand.

When Seamus was old enough to understand, sometime around the age of five, Susan did her best to explain to him why Colin was "different" and what those differences consisted of. Colin suffered from a malformation of his brain—in medical terms a partial agenesis of his corpus callosum, related to Turcot's syndrome, a rare inherited disorder. As newborns, there had been no noticeable difference between the boys. Then, at around four months, Colin, who had been capably holding a bottle and merrily feeding himself, suddenly lost the ability to do so. Other limitations began to emerge, and in the happy, playful Seamus there was a constant reminder that something was wrong with Colin. He was slower to learn most things. He had a lesser command of vocabulary and his enunciations were often a bit "off." The term for him in previous eras would have been "retarded," which was woefully nonspecific, not to mention unfair. Colin was able to achieve. But he had to work extremely hard to gain the small foothold that came so easily to others.

At school, Colin was "mainstreamed," meaning he attended regular age-appropriate classes, but was pulled out during the day for special education. When the twins began their schooling, they of course wanted to be in class together. But it was obvious that with Seamus around, Colin would never make much progress. Seamus would do all his tasks for him. It was a role that came naturally to him.

Seamus was quick to come to Colin's defense, and this soon expanded into a more generalized defense of any child who was teased or taunted for a reason that was essentially inherent, be it looks or dress or athletic shortcomings. "You know, that could be you," he would say. "Just an accident at birth and that could be you."

Laura Peters, one of Seamus's classmates, recalls her first memory of him. The children were at recess, and a group of boys was forming a kickball game. Laura knew Seamus only by reputation, as the "normal" twin, the one who didn't frequently shuttle to the resource room for special ed instruction, the one who spoke in clear, comprehensible sentences, the one who seemed lighthearted.

The boys choosing sides for kickball picked Seamus. Only if his brother could play, Seamus told them. The kickballers scoffed at this suggestion. Seamus said that if Colin couldn't play, then he wouldn't.

"That's the first real memory I have of him," said Laura. "Seamus didn't make a fuss. He just walked away to play somewhere else."

• • •

The discovery of Seamus's condition had a devastating effect on his parents. Jim immediately asked the state police to transfer him out of the sexual assault unit. His passion for helping kids in dire need was for the time being overextended. He was soon shifted to the white-collar crime unit, which he found boring but at least psychologically tolerable.

At night, Jim was haunted by disturbing dreams. In them, he was always losing control. He would be walking in a room and the carpet would suddenly give way, tumbling him endlessly downward into a void. He'd wake up perspiring, go check on the kids in their slumbering innocence, and not be able to fall asleep again. He began to develop a distinct stutter, particularly with the words *cancer* and *death*.

Susan and Jim felt a need—theirs and Seamus's—to be counseled by a religious figure. Both had been raised Catholic, but had strayed in recent years. Moreover, they were still reeling from an incident that had occurred a few days ago at the hospital.

Providence Medical Center was affiliated with the Catholic Church. The night before Seamus's surgery, Susan and Jim had encountered an elderly Catholic priest in the waiting room. They told him about their son, thinking that Seamus might be in need of spiritual counseling.

The priest heard them out and then began muttering a prayer, asking God to forgive Seamus's sins. Jim and Susan were appalled. To them, Seamus was an absolute innocent with nothing to apologize for and nothing to forgive. They promptly stood, without even telling the priest Seamus's room number, and walked away.

Still, it seemed negligent to not start bracing for the worst.

Susan had a friend who attended the First Presbyterian Church of Anchorage and spoke highly of their new minister, Dr. David Bleivik. Like other clergy, Bleivik made periodic visits to local hospitals, and Susan asked her friend to arrange a visit.

Dr. Bleivik had been in Alaska for about a year, having moved from a church in Chesapeake, Virginia. He was, on the surface, a somewhat contradictory figure, a devoutly religious man who was also palpably irreverent. Raised in Brooklyn, New York, he'd flirted with street gangs as a kid and came to the clergy after several years in U.S. Army intelligence during the Vietnam era (he was stationed in Europe).

Dr. Bleivik was a stocky man, slightly below average in height. He'd been told that he resembled the movie actor Steve McQueen, and he'd also been told that he resembled the TV actor Bob Newhart. He was keenly aware that there was a wide gap between the images projected by those two media stars—one intense and cunning, the other affable and wry. With Bleivik, each comparison was accurate—to a degree. He had what might be termed an approachable look on his face. He had a penchant for wearing brightly colored ties, as if to imply, without the risk of an overt declaration, that he was not exactly what one might expect of a religious figure.

Because he was neither stuffy nor sanctimonious, Bleivik quickly became known in communities where he was assigned as, in his words, "someone to call if somebody's in a bad way." He had an ability to bring calm and peace to those who were suffering or in turmoil. It was a "gift," according to many who'd been served by his efforts. Bleivik himself recoiled from using such a term. He was not the sort of religious figure who felt the need to dress up his reputation.

As a young minister in rural Virginia back when pain medication was less effective and less liberally prescribed than it is today, he would go visit people in tremendous pain—cancer victims, accident victims, victims of deliberate violence—and he would sit down by their bedsides. Sometimes their pain was so great they could barely acknowledge his presence through the wall of their agony. He would speak with them, pray, and try to connect, or at least communicate. He would do this regardless of the response he received. It was his purpose, he felt, to be present at the bedside of the suffering, and he would do what he could, reading, praying, talking in his steady voice laced with a Brooklyn accent.

And oftentimes a strange thing happened: Bleivik would glance up to discover that the agonized patient had mercifully fallen sound asleep.

An uncanny ability to put people to sleep in social settings was, he freely admitted, the stuff of jokes.

In his chosen line of work, however, it was a blessing.

• • •

One afternoon, Dr. Bleivik stopped by to meet Seamus. He was set to be released from Providence Medical Center the next day. "It was kind of awkward," Bleivik recalled. "I'd never met the family. They'd never met me. They're Catholic. I'm Presbyterian. I hardly even knew the woman who referred me. I really didn't know what to expect."

They chatted amiably. Bleivik asked Seamus what grade he was in. Fourth? Bleivik told him he'd been only a year older than that when he'd gotten kicked out of school for being part of a gang. This disclosure, stated matter-of-factly, had its desired effect. Seamus was eager to know more. What was it like, being in a gang? Why had he joined one? Why were they considered so bad?

Bleivik was happy to answer. He told a story about setting off cherry bombs in the fenced-in asphalt school yard and dashing away before he got caught. Or so he thought.

The rascal's glint in Seamus's eyes reminded Bleivik of some of his boyhood pals in the Bay Ridge neighborhood of Brooklyn back in the 1950s. "I'll tell you something," Bleivik said to Seamus. "If I had a gang now, I'd sure want you as a member. Because you're one very tough young man."

"Really?"

"Yes, really."

Bleivik spoke some about God, and how all that occurs is, ultimately, his work. He prayed with Seamus and his parents. Then he got up to leave. He'd done enough bedside counseling and hospital visits over the course of his career to be aware that you never knew exactly how you were being perceived by the suffering party. You might strike a rapport, or you might miss entirely. Bleivik's goal was simply to make available, as best as possible, the comfort that can come from faith in God. He was not a salesman. He had no interest vested in Seamus's response beyond wanting to alleviate the boy's misfortune. Rejection or acceptance, Bleivik did not take it personally. Nor did he view it as a vote for or against the Presbyterian system of belief for which he was an official representative. He'd done his best to relate to

Seamus. That was about all he could do. Not everybody reaches everybody, Bleivik told himself.

He held the boy's hand and, with Jim and Susan Farrell looking on, asked the only question that mattered at this stage. "Do you want me to come back?"

"Definitely," Seamus chirped. "That'd be great."

Bleivik was glad to hear it. He liked this kid.

Exiting the hospital in the pitch darkness of the late afternoon, four days before Christmas, Dr. Bleivik muttered angrily to himself, "This really stinks."

• • •

Seamus's actual medical diagnosis was: malignant astrocytoma. Because the tumor was located in the corpus callosum, deep in the center of his brain, it was considered inoperable. Soon after opening Seamus up, the surgeon, Dr. Lawrence Dempsey, had found necrotic (dead) tissue, another very bad sign. Thus, the typically slim survival chances of an astrocytoma patient were further reduced.

Dr. Dempsey referred Seamus for radiation treatment, to begin as soon as he was strong enough to withstand it. Even then, there was no expectation that he might live longer than a month or two. Radiation would be administered five days a week, beginning immediately after New Year's.

Seamus came home on December 22.

He seemed to be in good spirits. It was hard to know his inner thoughts. At his core, he was still a fun-loving ten-year-old. He and Colin and Jesse played with a Game Boy and watched videos, jostling each other and laughing. The one fear he did express was that he might lose his friends due to his illness. He had been briefed about the radiation therapy he would undergo and was worried kids wouldn't like him—or might be afraid of him—with his hair fallen out. Mostly, he was worried that his classmates would forget about him.

"Of course they'll remember you," Susan reassured him. It was the right thing to say, although she was privately dubious. Kids were kids. Time scoots by. Lives get busy. Distractions accumulate.

"Really, Mom?"

"Of course, they'll still be your friends."

Jim and Susan constantly forced themselves to be positive and cheerful, to act "normal" while their hearts were breaking. They did not want to further burden Seamus with having to see his parents morose or frightened.

Jim and Susan had no time, nor much inclination, to adorn the house with Christmas lights and wreaths or even a tree. But tomorrow, they promised themselves, they would go shopping to dress the house for the holiday. If this was to be Seamus's last Christmas, they wanted it to be like all the happy ones that had preceded it.

That evening there was a knock at the Farrells' front door. Susan answered and was met by half a dozen state troopers, some in uniform, some not, hoisting armloads of cookies, food, and presents of all shapes and sizes wrapped in colorful paper, enough to fill a six-foot patch of the living-room floor with a pile that was nearly as tall as Seamus.

And then they swept in with the finishing touch, a large, fragrant, symmetrical evergreen. Susan held open the door and the troopers romped in like the prancing chorus of a Broadway production, wisecracking, effusive, even singing. Seamus, of course, was the focal point of their attention, but there were gifts and jokes and good cheer for the entire household.

It was, Susan observed with unintended irony, just what the doctor ordered.

• • •

"Circle up," Elaine said. The children, newly returned from holiday break, gathered around. Outside the big windows, the January morning was dark and bitterly cold. Everyone felt the coziness of being huddled together again in Room 112.

Circle Time on the first day back after winter vacation was always lively. Everyone had two weeks' worth of stories to tell. Eagle River families often traveled to the Lower 48 to visit relatives, yielding enthusiastic accounts of first cousins who were so much fun, or an indoor zoo where a gorilla went crazy, or spending the entire night in the Minneapolis airport due to a cancelled flight. Kids who stayed in town had outdoor adventures to report—skiing at Alyeska, caroling with their church group.

"I want to tell you about Seamus," Elaine began. She had conferred with Susan and Jim, wanting to respect their wishes concerning what information to disclose. "Seamus is very ill."

"I thought his surgery was OK," said one boy.

"We thought it was," Elaine sighed. This was going to be difficult, but it was the right thing to do.

She had thought long and hard about how to approach this. In all probability this was going to be the children's first exposure to death. One of the side features of living in Alaska was that many families were cut off from elderly relatives. They had little experience with aged or dying grandparents. Not that there was a true comparison. Children think they are immortal. And why shouldn't they? The odds favor them. One of the wonderful benefits to being young is being able to plunge into the moment, the sweet center of here and now, like there's no tomorrow. Part of what allows kids to be kids is precisely this.

Facing up to Seamus's situation was bound to affect them. Ignoring his situation was not, Elaine believed, an option.

"Seamus has cancer, and we've learned it is very serious," she told the class. "He may not be able to come back to school."

The children froze. No squirming, no movement, no chatter, no noise. Seamus not coming back to class? Not popping through the door first thing in the morning and scrambling to find a place among them on the floor at Circle Time?

It didn't seem right. It didn't seem fair. And it didn't seem that there should be nothing at all that they could do about it.

"He is still part of our class," Elaine reassured them. It sounded like the right thing to say. But even as she said it, she had no clear notion of how this fact might be borne out. She only knew that the kids could not be cut off so abruptly from their bubbly classmate.

"He loves getting your notes," she added. "He knows how much you miss him."

"What happens if he dies?"

This one caught her by surprise. Elaine composed her answer carefully. "That is something each of you might want to talk about with your parents. People have different beliefs about that."

"But we'll get to see him again, won't we?"

This, she could see, was going to be one tricky balancing act, fulfilling her promise to be honest and yet somehow going onward with hope. "I hope so, yes. I'll find out more from his parents," she promised.

There was a lull in the classroom, which was not typical. A teaching colleague once asked, expressing some skepticism about Circle Time, "What happens when nobody has anything to say?"

"It's never happened," Elaine had answered bluntly. And that was true.

This lull did not last long. The kids, Elaine could tell, were thinking hard. "He's too sick to come to class, is that right?" someone asked.

"Yes, that's right."

"Can we visit him?"

"Yes, of course."

"I mean as a class, can we visit him?"

"Possibly," Elaine hedged. The reality, she recognized, would be more complicated. It was not her style to equivocate, but she could see where this might be going. The children were eager to do something. Such a response was natural. As a practical matter, however, they were fourth graders in a public school that operated under strict guidelines.

The activities of a Ravenwood Elementary classroom were not regulated in minute-by-minute details (thus, something as ostensibly nonacademic as Circle Time could be a daily feature of their lives). Yet there were a host of stipulations that governed how time was spent while children were under the direct supervision of the school—time allotted to reading, to math, to science, etc.—and there was a veritable mountain of curriculum goals to be met, week by week, in order to comply with statewide standards.

Schools, for all the improvised, unpredictable, seat-of-the-pants magic that so often constitutes the grand moments of learning, are famously bureaucratized environments. There is a chain of command nearly as explicit as that of the military and, like the military, it is underpinned by overarching notions of responsibility. "The buck stops here" is not quite the operative phrase in schools that it is in some other highly structured domains, but it is no less applicable. Teachers are answerable to principals who are answerable to superintendents who answer to community school boards who represent voters who elect mayors and governors. Jobs, careers, livelihoods are on the line, and the rules and regulations are explicitly codified in black and white to show that people in authority have judiciously created guidelines and set policies to implement them.

For there's no underestimating the magnitude of what is at stake: vulnerable children are entrusted to these schools for seven hours per day, more than 180 days per year over the course of thirteen or so years. During the course of the typical fall-winter-spring school calendar, many children spend nearly as much or more time at their school as they do with their parents.

"We will be a family this year, a school family," Elaine liked to tell her students at the start of the year. "We will be spending as much time with each other as we do with our real families."

So whatever gestures the kids might want to make toward Seamus, to help ease their sadness and his, protocol was involved. Schools have rules.

But so does the human heart.

Elaine prepared a letter for the parents. The letter was written in the same straightforward tone of the other missives the parents had received from her, related to teacher conferences or upcoming field trips. The note read:

Dear parents,

As you know, Seamus has an inoperable brain tumor.

I would like to begin talking with the children gently and honestly about his condition. I have excellent videos and books to help the children understand as well as open up lines of communication. A hospice volunteer will be available to speak to the students and help answer questions. My hope is that it will become an open topic of conversation in our classroom. We will spend a lot of time talking about our feelings and questions. Your child will need lots of support in coping with the classmate's terminal illness. But I believe children have an amazing ability and capacity to deal with the truth. Even sad truths relieve the anxiety of uncertainty.

This will be a learning opportunity for your child. I know from my own experience that when you learn about death you actually are learning about life.

Thank you for your continued support.

Sincerely,
Elaine Moore

Before running off copies of the note, Elaine paused to read it over. It looked OK. Yes, it made some references to Seamus's condition that might have been phrased differently. But she could not think of a better way to state it. Seamus didn't have long to live. The kids cared about him. Time was running out. That monumental fact had to be part of their class. How else to put it?

At the end of the afternoon, Elaine told the class that she had a letter to give to their parents: would they please put it in their backpacks and be sure to give it to their mother or father?

The bell rang. Kids grabbed their coats off the racks, yanked their caps from the sleeves, and tumbled out to the bus. Elaine sighed. The day was done. An important first step had been taken. There was no way to know exactly the right way to handle this. She had only her instincts to go on, her instincts about kids.

After school, Joan Johnson stopped by. Joan and Elaine were part of an informal group of teachers, imbued with ideas of outdoor education and eager to explore innovative ways of reaching children, who met after school once a week. It was a support group of sorts, where they could discuss their methods with colleagues who both understood what they were attempting and were engaged in trying out similar practices. They swapped stories and offered each other suggestions. Quality teachers in busy school situations often say that the biggest obstacle to being successful is the lack of opportunity to confer with colleagues. These regular meetings with her like-minded colleagues had proven over the years to be a lifeline for Elaine. She took great pride in what she did, and tried to do, in the classroom. Who else but another teacher could even begin to understand?

Elaine told Joan about the note. Joan urged her, if only to cover her bases, to show a copy to the principal. Elaine grumbled, but agreed that Joan was probably right.

Elaine walked down the corridor and found Arge Jeffery in his office. From his window, you could see the kids boarding the school buses beneath the gleaming flood-lights. Elaine handed Arge the letter, saying she wanted him to be aware of how she was handling the seriousness of Seamus's situation.

Arge was a stocky, balding, carefully dressed man with a neatly trimmed gray beard and a habit of jingling change in his pocket while he conversed. He was a stickler for institutional procedure. It was said that he was somewhat misplaced in education, and that he would have made a keen trial lawyer.

Elaine and Arge had their disagreements yet maintained a professional respect. She chafed at some of his bureaucratic ways, but understood he was ultimately responsible for governing a larger apparatus. Similarly, he wished Elaine were more conventional, but admired her skill with students. He quickly read the letter.

"What?" he bellowed. "Terminal? Elaine, you can't say a thing like that!"

"Arge," she replied, calmly dropping her voice to the level of a whisper, "he has *six weeks* to live."

"Well you can't use a word like *terminal* around kids."

"What word then? Tell me."

"I don't know, Elaine. Something like . . . like . . ."

She dared him to say it: something happier, more uplifting, something sugarcoated and optimistic?

He tossed the letter back. "Rewrite it!"

"The letter," Elaine quietly informed him, "has already gone home."

With that, she turned and went back to her room to pack up for the day.

LEARNING UNTIL THE DAY . . .

E laine's first teaching assignment was at Fort Churchill on Hudson Bay in northern Manitoba, where there was a joint Canadian–U.S. North American Aerospace Defense Command (NORAD) installation, as well as a NASA rocket range and a winter-survival training base for the military. It was the fall of 1962 and she was twenty years old. She had just graduated from Brandon Teachers College in southern Manitoba with an elementary teaching certificate. She was up for an adventure, and thought she knew a good deal when she saw one.

Fort Churchill was a northern outpost that made regions of Alaska look temperate by comparison. Temperatures in winter could dip as low as 50 degrees below zero, and the year-round *average* daily temperature was only 20 degrees. The surrounding landscape was mostly a rocky, barren tundra. Hudson Bay was a vast expanse of frigid open water, larger than the state of Texas, that eventually opened onto the Labrador Sea. It was a favorite home for beluga whales. The Churchill area shoreline was known as the "polar bear capital of the world." During fall and spring, school recess was often cancelled due to the presence of migrating yellowish-white white bears.

Fort Churchill had not been chosen as the location of a vital military base because of its scenery. Rather, it was directly on a flight path to the Soviet Union. In the years following World War II, this inhospitable environment— home to only about 150 permanent residents, not including the abundant wildlife—became the base of operations for some 4,500 flight pilots, officers, mechanics, and crew. The dependents of the men stationed there needed schooling. Assuming that it would be difficult, if not impossible, to recruit teachers to the region on the basis of its rich cultural opportunities and sumptuous lifestyle, the Canadian Department of Defense offered a different package to lure prospective teachers: agree to teach two years at Fort Churchill, and following that you got your pick of teaching assignments at one of the Canadian military's genuinely attractive installations in Europe.

Elaine, at that point in her life, had never traveled more than a few hours' drive from the farm where she'd been raised. The only people she had ever met from someplace truly distant were the three German prisoners of war that her family had housed for several months in the waning years of World War II. (This was another interesting story she would sometimes tell her students, when the topic of "accepting differences" arose.)

Fort Churchill was a shock. Flying in, staring out the airplane window at this boundless no-man's-land without houses or roads or any indication of civilization—well, "barren" was the only possible word for it.

The few trees were puny scrubs, no more than several feet high. Their denuded branches shivered in the icy gusts roaring off the bay. The town was unappealing. Its frame buildings looked to be in disrepair and were cloaked in exposed tar paper. The Hudson's Bay Company store, continuing its original purpose as the last chance to stock up for a thousand miles, still carried trapping gear and pelts. There was a brutal snap and screech to the wind—and this was only early autumn. She shivered at the prospect of spending the long, dark winter months in a place so desolate.

Thankfully, there was more to Fort Churchill than met the eye. The military base featured rows of constructed prefab buildings that were connected to each other by a well-maintained system of underground tunnels designed to enable the flow of human activity during the frequent "whiteout" conditions. The base had a bakery, a post office, a gift shop, a bowling alley, chapels, a 600-seat movie theater, a hospital, and a school. It was a company town, pure and simple.

Teachers were treated, if not like royalty, then at least commensurate with officers' rank. Elaine had use of all the base's recreational facilities and ate all meals in the lavish officers' mess. She sat at tables covered in starched linen cloths and was offered what seemed to her to be exotic dishes served by impeccably dressed waiters. It was more luxury, by a long shot, than she'd ever known. She felt like she was in a movie, or on another planet. Or both.

The people she met were outgoing, friendly, accommodating, inclusive. Her living quarters were located in a wing of the officers' barracks that housed a few hundred non-military personnel: teachers, health workers, and base-related technicians and specialists. All of them were cut off from family and friends. All of them were stuck there for a limited period of time. All had a job to do, and all had plenty of time left over after the day's work was done. The fact that they were stranded in a terrain that was a far cry from paradise was less significant than the fact that they were stranded there together.

There was one other unmistakable feature about life at Fort Churchill. Almost everyone was male. And not just your average North American male, but heart-of-the-Cold-War-era military guys, imbued with lofty notions of patriotic duty and stuck a long, long way from the bright lights of town. The ratio was roughly this: 35 single women, 5,000 men. To say that Elaine, literally just off the farm, with her red hair, pleasant good looks, congenial manner, and hint of subdued femininity attracted suitors would be an understatement.

Guys of all shapes and sizes and sensibilities were everywhere, and it was suddenly obvious: there was absolutely nothing about the place that was isolating except its location on the map. She met her husband there, as did many of the imported teachers. (Few of the female teachers, as it turned out, stayed unmarried long enough to cash in on the promise of an attractive European posting; Elaine never got overseas until many years later.)

On October 22 of that year, President John F. Kennedy informed the world that the Soviet Union was building secret missile bases in Cuba, a mere ninety miles off the shores of Florida. Thus began what history books refer to as the Cuban Missile Crisis, a period of some fourteen days when the world came closer to the dreaded reality of all-out nuclear war than it hoped to ever again. The NORAD base at Fort Churchill was put on maximum, ready-to-launch alert.

After weighing various options, such as an invasion of Cuba and air strikes against the missiles, Kennedy decided to demand that Russian premier Nikita Khrushchev remove all missile bases and their contents from Cuba. Kennedy ordered a naval blockade of Cuba. In response, Khrushchev authorized Soviet field commanders in Cuba to launch their tactical nuclear weapons if invaded by U.S. forces. Deadlocked, the two nuclear superpowers famously stared each other down, each one daring the other to blink.

At Fort Churchill, red alert meant the B-52s were moved onto the runways, flight crews aboard, engines running twenty-four hours a day to be able to instantly take off without a second's delay should the order come down.

The school was adjacent to the airfield. The windows in Elaine's classroom vibrated from the revving jet engines. She found herself having to shout above the heavy roar to be heard. Even second graders, the level she was teaching in this, her first official year, understood that the drama unfolding was like no other. Those planes outside preparing to launch contained their fathers.

It was a strain for Elaine to keep the youngsters' attention focused on their reading, arithmetic, and handwriting. The classroom, Elaine had once thought, should be an oasis, isolated as much as possible from the shortsighted distractions of everyday events. At the military base school at Fort Churchill, Manitoba, in October 1962, there was no holding back the angry intrusions of the larger world. Elaine could only do her best to talk over the roar.

● ● ●

That first week back at school, Elaine showed a video to the class that the Ravenwood librarian had recommended. It was titled *Why, Charlie Brown, Why*, and featured familiar characters from the *Peanuts* series.

The video begins with kids waiting for the morning bus. The leaves on the trees are turning red. It's fall. Janice, a girl with bright yellow hair, bruises herself as she gets on the school bus and complains to her seatmate that she still has bruises from bumps she suffered last week.

Outside on the playground, Linus wants to push Janice on the swing, but she doesn't feel well and declines. In school that day, Janice has a stomachache and feels tired. Janice is sent home. We see her outside the school, all alone, waiting for her mother to pick her up.

Linus and Charlie Brown, her classmates, learn that Janice has been hospitalized. After school, they head to the hospital and find her lying in bed with an IV tube attached to her arm.

"I have cancer," she tells them.

"Are you going to die?" Linus blurts out.

Charlie scolds him, but Janice says, "That's all right. I asked the same question." She describes what she's been undergoing, the bone marrow test (for leukemia), the CAT scan, the chemotherapy.

As they say good-bye, Janice says to them, "I'm going to get well and swing on those swings."

Then it's winter. Playing outside, Janice is teased by a boy who mocks her bald head. Charlie has harsh words for him, pointing out how brave Janice is for all that she's endured.

Green leaves return to the trees. It's spring and Janice comes back to school. Linus pushes her on the spring and— whoosh!—her cap flies off and we see her hair, yellow and flowing and full once again.

Bouncy music. Fade-out. The end, and a happy one.

"I hope Seamus gets better," someone said when the video was over.

"Like Janice."

"With brown hair."

"I didn't mean the hair color."

• • •

Seamus, meanwhile, was having a hard time of it. He'd started intensive radiation therapy, five days per week. It was extremely debilitating and all but vanquished his remaining appetite. At this time, he was put on Decadron and dexamethasone to relieve swelling in his skull. A side effect was a tremendous increase in his appetite. Every day after radiation, Susan would take him by a Taco Bell, where he'd wolf down half a dozen tacos with soda.

The family tried to establish a semblance of normalcy. Jesse and Colin returned to Ravenwood and were quickly absorbed in the busy rhythms, respectively, of sixth and fourth graders. Joseph resumed his studies at the University of Alaska–Anchorage. Susan, whose days were now filled with outpatient hospital visits and the ongoing panic of exploring every single medical option that might conceivably save Seamus, put her nursing studies on hold.

Dr. Bleivik paid a visit to the Farrells' home, along Eagle River Road. Pulling his car into their driveway on a blustery January afternoon, it struck him that he was looking forward to seeing Seamus. He genuinely liked this boy and enjoyed their time together. Seamus had a way of laughing with carefree glee at, for example, Bleivik's joke about planting a cherry bomb in the school yard. An instant later, Seamus's face could turn almost beatific with the earnestness of a choirboy. That, Bleivik reflected, was a package he could relate to.

Bleivik brought Seamus a gift of several alien-themed comic books he'd picked up at Bosco's, a low-overhead novelty shop on the Old Glenn Highway. He had been told that Seamus was partial to monsters and aliens. This attraction to otherworldly creatures was something of a puzzle to Bleivik. He assumed it was an updating of what in his boyhood had been simple affection for dogs or horses or mice like Mickey. Are aliens a good thing for human civilization, or a threat? Would you like to have one for a friend? Bleivik guessed these questions were at the root of kids' interest in such creatures, but he could be wrong. It would give him something to talk about with Seamus—something other than the obvious.

At this point in his ministerial career, Bleivik had spent time, hard time, with at least several hundred people who were dying. He would never want to call it his specialty. But he knew he was good at it. Some years back he'd attended a workshop conducted by Elisabeth Kübler-Ross, the renowned advocate of patient-centric ways of dealing with death.

One of her demonstrations had made a lasting impression. Using a celluloid overlay that projected onto a large screen, Kübler-Ross had shown the audience a picture of a small boy. A cannon was aimed directly at the boy, and a cannonball in midair was heading his way. People attending the workshop were asked to imagine what they could draw onto this picture that would help comfort the terrified boy.

"A rainbow shooting from the gun," someone offered.

"That," stated Kübler-Ross, "would be a lie."

"A concrete wall," someone suggested. "To stop the bullet."

"Uh uh. Another lie. It won't happen."

With no better answers forthcoming, Kübler-Ross went to the projector. With brisk strokes, she sketched onto the celluloid overlay the answer she believed was the right and only one.

She drew a picture of a human hand reaching out to hold the child's hand.

• • •

Bleivik was happy to shoot the breeze with Seamus. "He was," he noted, "just a real fun kid." Yet there was another agenda, and it could not be forever brushed aside with banter about aliens and football and Sonic the Hedgehog (another favorite). Bleivik felt he had to begin readying the boy for his death. "I wanted," he said, "to be one more person holding his hand."

Partly to divert Seamus but also to figuratively hold his hand—the two were not separable—Bleivik told another anecdote, this one about his time serving in army intelligence. It was 1968 and Bleivik, who'd enlisted with the full expectation of going to Vietnam, had been assigned to Germany as part of the U.S. military's heightened focus on Europe in the aftermath of the Soviet invasion of Czechoslovakia. The future he saw for himself at that time was that he would serve out his army hitch, then join the FBI or another investigative branch of law enforcement. The ministry was not even an afterthought.

Bleivik's army intelligence duties included cultivating sources—"snitches," he called them, causing Seamus to smile at the minister's use of cop-show lingo. Bleivik had told this story many times, for it touched on a matter about which everyone was curious: namely, how did he come to be a man of God? For people of other professions, the question might well never come up. Law? Science? Sports? People assumed they knew why somebody might choose such paths. But not with the ministry.

The setup was this: Bleivik was "running" a snitch with the hope of discovering information about sectarian black militants. The snitch got involved with drugs and spilled the beans of his involvement with Bleivik, who was then suspected of being both a spy and a narc.

An angry soldier confronted Bleivik and menacingly dangled a single black leather glove in his face. "Know what this means?"

"Funny, but I lost a glove, too," said Bleivik, pretending not to understand the threat he'd just been issued.

"I could take you out with one hand," the soldier snorted.

"Probably could," Bleivik replied self-effacingly. The guy was half a foot taller than him, and meaner. "So could my little sister."

"You weren't afraid?" Seamus asked.

In truth, Bleivik had been terrified. He couldn't sleep at night, listening for prowlers outside his door. He lay in bed with a tight roll of pennies bunched in his fist to fortify that punch he knew he was soon going to be forced to throw. And lying there in bed, waiting for terror to burst through the door, he had the first deep conversation with God that he'd had in quite some time. It was a back-and-forth conversation. God, according to Bleivik, insisted on knowing what he was going to do with his life.

Law enforcement was Bleivik's answer.

Neither God nor he was persuaded. Trembling in fear, hoping to make peace with the Lord before an assailant came crashing in on him, Bleivik blurted out, "OK, God! I'll become a minister."

"And suddenly," he told Seamus, "I was no longer afraid."

"Not at all?"

"Not at all."

"Wow."

Later, as Jim escorted him to his car, Bleivik asked, "How are you handling this?"

"Frankly, I feel like telling God to go to hell."

"I do too sometimes," Bleivik told him. "He can take it."

• • •

In class, Seamus was a constant topic. During free time, when the children had completed their curriculum work, they enjoyed making cards for him. Elaine would periodically stop by the Farrells' house to deliver them.

"Oh, no, Seamus!" Jim would bellow in mock warning. "Your teacher's here!"

At Circle Time, she told the kids about the radiation treatments Seamus was receiving. Radiation, she explained, was the main treatment for brain tumors. Special equipment, an X-ray machine, was used to deliver high doses of radiation to prevent cells from growing in the cancerous tumor.

Naturally, the kids were curious to know if radiation really could cure cancer. Elaine could only say yes, it sometimes had that power. She had undergone extensive chemotherapy herself and here she was, two years later.

However, she cautioned, Seamus's tumor was among the most serious types and, located where it was within his brain, among the most difficult to effectively treat. His chances weren't good, but she could not bring herself to say that Seamus actually had no chance. There was always hope.

The second week after holiday break, Seamus came to visit. Elaine had told Susan that he should come, on whatever basis, at whatever time suited him. She wanted it understood—by Susan and by Seamus—that he would continue to be a member of the class. Seamus had completed two weeks of radiation therapy and, while feeling far from peppy, was learning that some days were better than others. One morning he told his mother that the thing that would make him most happy would be a trip to Ravenwood School.

Seamus had been a popular boy long before he became an object of sympathy. He was spunky and playful, but also sensitive, and he didn't care who knew it. After watching the movie *Jaws*, he was upset at the decision to destroy the giant shark. "He [the shark] could have been trained to be good," he'd protested. "They didn't have to kill him." The special qualities he brought to the class were missed.

Seamus could walk, but only unsteadily. He had developed a severe foot drop, a worsening of the limp and purported ankle injury that had afflicted him back in the innocent fall, and he wore a hard plastic brace on his bad leg for support. Otherwise, it could have been the same old Seamus. Elaine had done little specifically to prepare the class for this visit—but then again, they'd been preparing all school year.

Seamus sat in a chair. Kids gathered around him. There was a moment's hesitation as his emotions adjusted to being back in this cozy space, with its wall maps and artwork and large-lettered sign above the door: THIS ROOM IS A SAFE PLACE.

Seamus sat there beaming. He wore a blue U.S. Navy cap with gold lettering.

"Nice hat," someone said.

"Usually I keep it on," he told them. Much of his hair

had fallen out. What remained was aggregated in a few isolated clumps, as if it had been erratically pasted on as a Mr. Potato Head project. It looked scary.

"Does it hurt?" a classmate wanted to know.

"No," he told them. "Radiation doesn't hurt."

But, he told them, if they hadn't put him to sleep and given him pain pills it sure would've hurt when they cut his skull open!

The kids grimaced. "They *cut your skull open?*"

"Sure. Want to see?"

He removed his cap and rotated his bare scalp first this way, then that, so all the kids could see the suture line carved in a large horseshoe shape above his left ear.

He sipped some hot chocolate. "This is good for me," he said, lifting the cup.

He talked about the severe headaches he got and the medication he took that didn't always work. He talked about his radiation therapy, how he got to drink hot chocolate in the waiting room beforehand and what they did to him.

Watching this, Elaine was dazzled by Seamus's openness in sharing his trauma with his classmates. The easy flow of this get-together was so unlike her own experience with adults in the aftermath of her cancer. Then, people might see her coming down the aisle at the grocery store and veer away to avoid having to . . . having to what? Think about it? Make small talk about it? Put their pity into words? Confront their own mortality? Simply say they were sorry?

She knew it wasn't that people didn't care. They were

simply hung up, unlike children, about what to say, or what not to say.

It was a little like show-and-tell, with Seamus, seated in a chair in the circle, in charge of the presentation. What he'd brought to show and tell about was himself. He told the kids he'd been worried before the surgery, but that his family had all been there and that that had made him feel better. He told how he'd met the surgeon and he was a very nice man, and how that had made him feel better also. He talked of how the surgeon cut into his skull and looked at his brain.

Some kids were wide-eyed. Some flinched at the very thought of it. Most were fascinated by every detail.

"It didn't hurt because I was asleep," he assured them.

He talked about his stay in the hospital and the visit from the marines in full uniform who called him "brave and courageous." He did not mention Miss Alaska, for that would have caused him to blush all over again. But he did mention the mysterious little girl who anonymously deposited a giant white teddy bear in his room.

Elaine had planned to have a lesson today on People Who Make a Difference, in conjunction with the upcoming Martin Luther King Day holiday. Ravenwood, like schools throughout the country, honored Martin Luther King's mid-January birthday in various ways. The school library displayed several biographies of King right by the main desk. Posters of King captioned by iconic phrases from famous speeches—JUDGED NOT BY THE COLOR OF OUR

SKIN BUT THE CONTENT OF OUR CHARACTER—hung in several classrooms.

Elaine sought ways to honor Dr. King by widening the topic. The lesson to be learned from his life, she felt, was not necessarily that a heroic Nobel Peace Prize winner lionized in story and song was a man of noble purpose. Everyone knew that. A better lesson, and one perhaps truer to King's spirit, was to stress how one person's deeds—a person who is not famous, not legendary, not the most spectacular at this or most extraordinary at that, a regular person who is unheralded yet virtuous—can have a profound impact.

Such a person did not have to create a huge wave or generate a storm. A ripple could suffice. Few of us, she pointed out, ever get to personally meet the Martin Luther Kings of the world. But we all know people who make positive contributions to the greater good. We just need to refocus our definition.

"Who could that be in your world?" she asked them. "Your sister? Your brother?"

She paused for the predictable chuckling.

"Maybe someone at church or your next-door neighbor?"

She could see them chewing on this. To encourage the discussion, and the writing assignment that would eventually derive from it, Elaine liked to tell her students about somebody they'd never heard of, somebody who would certainly never be written about in any books, yet a person who'd nonetheless made a difference in her life.

She told them about the winter's night when she was a girl and her father had just come home unexpectedly early from the all-important Manitoba Bonspiel.

"A what, Mrs. Moore?"

"A bonspiel. You're telling me you never heard of a bonspiel?" She knew they probably hadn't.

"A bon what?"

Brimming with Canadian pride, she outlined the sport of curling. She told them about the rock, a freeze, the hack, heavy ice, and sweeping. Her story had to do with the rules. Curling had no umpires or referees. It was a competitive sport conducted on the personal honor system.

Her father had been an acclaimed curler. That day at the competition, which Elaine characterized for the kids as being something akin to the Olympics of curling, his opponents had tried a deceitful tactic. To understand what happened, she told them about the hog line.

"The what?"

"You don't know what a hog line is?" she laughed. Explaining the components of a sport to someone who's never seen it played requires dexterity, and not just with words. Elaine stood in the space by the windows and gave a quick demo of basic curling moves.

The hog line is painted on the ice, like the blue line in hockey. The "hack" is where the curler places his foot before delivering the stone. Due to deteriorated ice conditions, her father's team and their opponent had agreed to relocating the hack by a few feet . . . Then, once her father's team moved well into the lead, the opposing team protested the revised placement of the hack.

"This was the biggest competition of the year," Elaine told the kids, "and do you know what my father did?"

"What?"

"He turned his back and walked off the ice."

"He just quit?"

"That's not how he saw it." He saw it, Elaine explained, as doing the right thing. Honor and sportsmanship were paramount to him. The merest suggestion that he would do anything dishonorable filled him with disgust. Anyone who would cheat or even attempt to cheat, as this other team had, was beneath his contempt. It did not matter to him that this was a championship competition. It did not matter that his team was still in a position to win. Sportsmanship. Honor. Your word. That's what mattered to him more than anything else.

"His favorite expression," she told the kids, "was 'Play 'er fair and square.' That was the motto he lived by."

She could see that the kids did not exactly get it.

"Play the game, every game—and that includes school—fair and square. Do your best and never cheat, not yourself or anyone else. That's what he meant. 'Play 'er fair and square.'"

Her father had been a hardworking, charismatic man with talents that never quite paid off. He might have benefited by taking a few shortcuts, dodging a few onerous responsibilities.

But that had not been his style. Play 'er fair and square. That was Reg Westcott's style.

"Would you say he made a difference?" she asked.

"Sure, Mrs. Moore. To you."

Susan had been waiting outside in the corridor, chatting with teachers and staff passing by. For her, this was a rare interlude of buoyancy, knowing Seamus was in there with his friends. Glancing in now, she could see that he was beginning to flag. His hand gestures, as animated as a New York City traffic cop when he'd first arrived, had slowed down. Her biggest fear was that he might collapse or begin vomiting, which would cause him embarrassment.

She scooted in, holding his coat, and announced in a brisk, motherly voice that it was time to go. Seamus did not argue. He gave a good-bye wave and started for the door with his mother's arm around his shoulder.

"Will you come again?" several children asked.

"You bet!"

• • •

Where the idea first came from, nobody is sure.

Elaine, true to form, insists it was not hers but grew organically from Circle Time the way fertile soil soaked by rain will mushroom with varied forms of growth. The seeds, after all, were always there in latent form.

Classmates vaguely remember kicking the idea around, but whether that was the origin of the suggestion or simply a fragmented recollection of subsequent efforts to develop it, no one can say.

The idea was this: if Seamus was no longer strong enough to come to Ravenwood, why not have the class come to him at home?

Transporting nearly thirty children off campus during school hours raised a host of logistical as well as administrative issues. You'd need a bus. You'd need chaperones. You'd need to usurp time allocated for curriculum matters. You'd need parental permission. Plus, you would need some way to justify it beyond the fact that Seamus was a nice kid who was dying.

Hans, or maybe it was Alex Vanderhoff, or possibly Paul Hackenmueller or Laura Peters, pointed out that they could make it, well, like a field trip. Mrs. Moore was famous for taking her classes on so many field trips. Just substitute Seamus Farrell's home for Chugach State Park or the Native Village of Eklutna or the historical museum. Was there any rule that stipulated a school field trip had to be to some woodsy, outdoor, ultradifferent kind of environment?

The kids wanted to know if there was any reason a field trip *had to be* to a place that you would never go to casually? Couldn't a field trip be just as rewarding, just as educational, just as fulfilling, without a destination that was exotic or far away?

The kids hurled these questions at Elaine as if she—of all people!—were the very embodiment of education officialdom. She patiently heard them out. It was not her style to quash an idea in its nascent stage. This one, however, she could see bumping into a brick wall.

"What if . . ." Mrs. Moore was thinking aloud.

Everyone paused. Elaine had been shaking her head "no," but she'd stopped doing that. There was a look that came over her when a promising notion was percolating in its formative stage. Her eyes would assume an abstract, far-away, unfocused gaze, as if she were observing nothing more concrete than color and light. She was not a nail-biter, but her thumb would push up to her mouth.

"What if," she asked, "we did it at lunchtime?"

Whoa. Now we're talking. Right away, the kids saw the possibilities. Lunch hour circumvented several obstacles. But several more remained.

"How're we all going to fit?" one child wanted to know.

"The bus has plenty . . ."

"Not the bus. His house. How many'll fit in his house?"

The boy had a point. Their elation ebbed.

"But," Elaine offered, "if we visited Seamus in small groups . . ."

This met with a mixed reception. Already, their broad vision was being compromised. However, the idea had a viability in this compromised form.

Elaine went to speak with the principal. She could anticipate Arge's objections and knew they had validity. He'd want to know: What happens if Seamus dies while the kids are at his house? How was he supposed to handle parents if that happened? Emotional damage? Psychological scars? Those were concepts that in the hands of a shrewd attorney could be attached to hefty sums of money—very hefty indeed. And what about precedent? What if another child at Ravenwood—or elsewhere in the district—were to be stricken with a terminal illness? Would they feel they were entitled to similar treatment?

Elaine patiently presented her plan to Arge. All visits would take place during lunch hour and recess. She would tell the parents what this was about and ask their permission. Any parent who did not want their child participating would, of course, have their wish respected. She would have the kids visit Seamus in small groups of three or four and would enlist parent volunteers to drive and chaperone.

Arge heard her out, jingling his pocketful of change. When she'd concluded, he said, "Absolutely not."

She persisted, stressing the importance of community to her class, and how much it mattered to the kids to maintain it. Continuing their relationship with Seamus, and keeping him involved, was not a secondary matter to them. It was, Elaine insisted, at the heart of everything she was trying to do.

Arge admired Elaine, although her unorthodox methods could grate on him. Sensing some acquiescence, she told him more of the plan.

In the weekly newsletter home, she would describe the idea and promise to keep the parents apprised of every step of the project. She would emphasize that schoolwork would be the focus of the visits to Seamus, and that the kids would be going to his house in the spirit of tutoring him about the classwork he was missing. Indeed, it was her belief that this would be a tremendous motivator, for who would want to let Seamus down by not knowing enough to effectively teach him? Peer tutoring, it was called. It was the soul of good learning and it was, harkening back to her one-room schoolhouse in Douglas, the impetus for her own career as a teacher.

The kids, she emphasized to Arge, were desperate to prevent Seamus from falling behind. They wanted him to keep pace. That way, and only that way, could he remain a member of the class.

She waited for Arge's response.

"Well . . ." Maybe Arge was better suited to being a lawyer, as some contended. But education was where he'd made his commitment. "OK," he said. "OK, Elaine."

• • •

Elaine wrote a new note to be brought home by the kids.

Dear parents,

The students and I have come up with a plan to help Seamus keep up with our classroom activities. Once or twice a week, three or four students will visit Seamus at home to help him with his missed work. The students will take a sack lunch, leaving at 11:30 and returning at 12:30. They will be transported by parents and will be supervised by the parent and Mrs. Farrell for that time (Seamus lives very close to Ravenwood).

I think this is a wonderful opportunity for all of us. Thank you for your support.

Sincerely,
Elaine Moore

At the bottom of the note was a box to be checked. "Yes, my child has permission to travel by car to Seamus's home for extended learning," was written next to the box. A signature line lay below.

Every family signed.

• • •

Shortly after noon, a car containing several fourth graders and a parent-driver pulled into the Farrells' seventy-yard-long driveway. It was a split-entry-style home with a basic L shape that conformed to the incline on which it was situated. The three-bedroom, two-bath house was built in the mid-1970s during a period when Eagle River was in a growth spurt.

The Farrell home was located on a half-acre lot along Eagle River Road, which, as with most roads named in a similarly straightforward manner, roughly traces the course of the river. If there is a distinctive feature about the road, it is that the surrounding mountains are so precipitous and high— scaling thousands of feet at angles approaching 90 degrees up to peaks glistening with ice and snow even in mid-July—that the valley is almost its own self-contained world.

Eagle River Road winds its way to the head of the glacier, terminating in a dead end several miles past the Farrells'. The stretch of road where the Farrells lived, less than a mile from Ravenwood, is marked by houses not unlike what you would find in any middle-class subdivision of any suburban community anywhere in North America. Except these homes are surrounded by constant visual reminders that this is Alaska. Backyards disappear upward past the property line into a sloping no-man's-land of thickly forested mountainside. Susan Farrell used to enjoy gazing from her bedroom window at mountain sheep grazing on distant bluffs. There is only one road into this portion of the valley, and the same road leads out.

The parent-driver this day was Terry Simpson. A tall, blonde woman with a congenial manner and an angular set to her jaw and cheekbones, Terry was a uniformed street cop with the Anchorage police department, assigned to the Eagle River area. Her son Jake was friendly with Seamus and she knew Jim Farrell, although only casually, through overlapping duties on local cases that involved the Alaska state troopers.

Like other classroom parents, Terry had received the note from Elaine presenting the idea of regular lunch-hour visits to Seamus. By this time, everyone knew his circumstances. There was no need to rehash the bleak medical prognosis. Ravenwood had always been known as a school with strong parental involvement. The administration and the teachers encouraged this reputation for all the obvious benefits, from field-trip assistance to school pride to basic reinforcement of curricular goals.

Parental involvement was also a direct outgrowth of the type of people who settled here. They were largely middle-class, with a firm appreciation for the value of education. Eagle River families often found in the local public schools the tethering bonds of community that people in the Lower 48 enjoy in the form of blood relations or church groups or neighborhood affiliations dating back decades. In Eagle River, the school community often proved the best way to meet people, make friends, swap stories, arrange car pools, seek information on everything from doctors to car mechanics, and virtually anything else that might benefit your family or someone you knew. And the locus of this simple, busy, textured, back-and-forth exchange was the school your children attended. And therefore it felt like your school, too.

"You couldn't work at Ravenwood," noted Barbara Bernard, a curriculum specialist and mother of Seamus's classmate Hans, "if you didn't want parents looking over your shoulders."

Elaine's letter home informing parents that Seamus's cancer was considered "terminal" had excited more than a few curbside conversations at school bus stops and grocery stores. There had been concern, and even alarm, that a boy as deathly ill—a horrible phrase, but how else to say it?—as Seamus was being brought to school to sit among the kids and talk about his illness.

But the Room 112 parents were witnessing something else. Their children were coming home in the afternoons talking, talking, talking about Seamus and what they had learned, about him and from him. "We would talk about life and death at the dinner table," said Darlene Whitehead, mother of Danielle. "Lots of times when death is approaching, people close the doors and shut kids out. This time the door was open."

• • •

Terry Simpson was already in the habit of volunteering to help on her days off. She had seen how much this meant to her son Jake, a brown-haired boy with prominent cheekbones and dark, handsome eyes. Jake, like many other kids, had come home that day and told his mom every detail he could recall—and he could recall quite a lot—about Seamus's surgery and the ordeal of radiation and the enigmatic little girl who'd snuck into his hospital room while he was sound asleep and left a giant stuffed bear for him, just to be nice. Terry was happy to help with the lunch-hour shuttle.

In addition to Jake, Terry ferried three other children in her car: Alex Vanderhoff, a serious girl with thick, curly hair that had a tendency to fall in ringlets over her eyes; Austin (AJ) Pederson, a feisty, athletic boy who shared an impish smile and many interests with Seamus; and Danielle Whitehead, pretty, freckled, a meticulous dresser.

The kids signed up in groups of three or four. Elaine was in charge of selecting the delegations that would visit Seamus. Three visits per week was their aim. There was no set rotation governing who went on what day and with whom. What struck Elaine was that everyone wanted to go as often as possible. It was evident that their desire to visit Seamus and assist in his continued learning was a tool she could apply to *their* learning.

To make certain that Seamus understood what they were covering in class, they, as peer-tutors—for that's what they were—needed to be qualified for the job. To really help Seamus, they needed to be up to speed.

To understand long division well enough to show Seamus how it was done, they had to understand the concept of twelve being the same as three groups of four. To appreciate the contribution of native Alaskan peoples to the culture of Alaska, they had to grasp, at least somewhat, the anthropology of North America and how it came to be settled. To do right by Seamus, to not let him down, each child had to be equipped. Elaine did not have to spell it out for them; the kids readily got it.

Every child would get a chance to go. But if they'd done poorly on a quiz or homework assignment, or if they just didn't get the lesson, which could happen, especially with math, Elaine would ask them directly, "Do you really feel you understand this well enough to help teach it to Seamus?"

It was the honor system, play 'er fair and square. Nobody had any doubt about the value Mrs. Moore placed on the honor system.

"Maybe not," a child would sheepishly reply.

"Do you think if you worked a little harder, you could be ready to help him next week?"

"Yes, Mrs. Moore. Definitely."

One student, Erik Johnson, had moved into the Ravenwood district only after Christmas. He did not know Seamus. As Circle Time discussions increasingly touched on Seamus and the class grew more excited about the lunchtime "field trips," Erik became caught up in his classmates' enthusiasm. He worried that he would not be eligible.

One day he pulled Elaine aside. If he worked really hard at his lessons, Erik wanted to know, could he too be included in a visit to Seamus's house?

• • •

Jake, Alex, Danielle, and AJ tumbled out of Terry Simpson's marked blue and white Chevrolet Caprice. It was February. Snow was everywhere. Many feet had fallen since the first dusting back in September, and there'd been scarcely any melt. Sidewalks and driveways, sculpted by motorized snow blowers, had become steep canyons with high walls of packed snow and ice. The kids, bundled in bulky coats and caps, had the look of missionaries bringing offerings as they trudged toward the Farrells' front door.

Polite children, they knocked, although there was hardly any need to. Once inside, they removed their shoes like all good Alaskans, sensitive to the slush and salt and muck that would otherwise be tracked in.

The common entrance to the Farrell home was at the landing between the first level and the top-floor living area. The lower bedrooms were on the same level as the garage. Joseph and Jesse had their bedrooms there. When Seamus became ill, Colin moved in with Jesse. The stairway went immediately up to the second floor, which had an integrated kitchen/dining/living room area, a master bedroom, and what was formerly the twins' room but was now exclusively occupied by Seamus.

"Here they are!" Susan called out to Seamus.

On the day of his classmates' visits, he would be eagerly waiting in the living room. "It was," said Susan Farrell, "the absolute highlight of his day. Every time, it was the highlight."

For those who had not seen Seamus since his last visit to Ravenwood, it was a shock seeing him now. A side effect of taking heavy doses of the steroid dexamethasone to relieve the swelling was a great surge in eating. By late winter, Seamus's entire appearance had been transformed. His weight had exploded from a lithe forty-seven pounds to over a hundred pounds—and rising. Where there had previously been a little rascal's gauntness to his features, he was now a pumpkin. His face was pillowlike, puffed to dimensions that were almost perfectly round. His rosy cheeks and chin protruded and glistened. His eyes, while still blue and clear, were sunk in a deep cushion of flesh, their sparkle muffled and dimmed.

Elaine had warned the children of this transformation, and they'd come prepared.

"Seamus," they called up to him as they kicked off their boots and stripped off their coats and climbed up the stairs.

He used a walker to get around the house and he leaned on it now, watching his classmates.

Seeing him, they called, "How you doing, Seamus?"

"Come on in," he said and, sliding his walker forward, ushered them into the dining area, which was adjacent to the kitchen and living room. He wore a white and gold U.S. Coast Guard cap, one of his ever-expanding collection, which now numbered more than two dozen hats.

"There was always this little dance at first to figure out how he was feeling," said Hans Bernard. "If he was OK, we'd try to get down to schoolwork sooner. If not . . ."

This day, Seamus seemed pretty good. At least he was able to stand and walk slowly. The radical increase in his body weight had wreaked havoc on the ability of his weakened legs to support him.

The kids arranged themselves around the dining table, opening up their sandwich bags—cream cheese, peanut butter, ham and cheese—and spilling out some potato chips. Seamus, who seemed always to be eating, joined them with his favorite meal, what he termed a Bear Sandwich: peanut butter and honey on thickly sliced bakery bread that contained cottage cheese, dill, and pureed carrot. At the outset it was just kid banter, about TV shows or sporting events or recent movies like *Aladdin* or *Home Alone 2*.

As the kids munched, Seamus peppered them with questions.

He was intensely curious about the humdrum happenings at school. If kids reported they'd been to art class that morning, he wanted to know who drew what. He wanted to hear about the book Mrs. Moore was reading, what *part* she'd read that day, and what *happened* in that part of the book? Had Mrs. Moore brought any neat new bones to class? The study of bones was part of the fourth-grade science curriculum. They were supposed to learn the scientific names for the bones in the human body and understand their functions. Elaine had a bona fide skeleton hanging—yes, hanging!—in the room during the bone unit weeks and she taped thick hospital X-rays depicting broken femurs, clavicles, tibias, and fibulas to the windows. She loved to hear the kids using their newly acquired vocabulary, not necessarily to show off but for the pure sound-effect surprise. "I hurt my patella," a girl might say. Or, "I jammed my phalanges," a word that made a much greater impact than "finger."

What about gym? Seamus wanted to know what game they were playing in gym. Even if there'd been a fire drill, the most routine of all school routines, he'd want to know what it was like.

"Like they always are."

"Cool," he'd say. "No fire?"

"Of course no fire."

"Any field trips coming up?"

"You're our field trip, Seamus."

"That's great," he'd laugh. "How about celebrations? Any new celebrations?" Seamus loved inventing celebrations.

In fact, the class had discussed ideas for making a celebration around Seamus—Day Seamus Came Back to Class Day. But the discussion was left unresolved, largely because, well, Seamus's situation was so unresolved. Anyway, there was always the chance of truly astonishing developments down the road that would leave no doubt in anyone's mind about the prime opportunity for a Seamus-themed celebration.

Then it was time for schoolwork.

The group cleaned up their wrappers and juice and brought out their papers. The first order of business was correcting Seamus's work sheets. Each delegation would bring learning activities to Seamus. These were the same curriculum-related questions that the class was working on, involving math and history and science. They worked on these together, explaining the finer points to Seamus.

Elaine largely disdained fill-in-the-blank workbook assignments, preferring that the kids grapple with more open-ended questions that might, with the exception of math, lack a single, precise answer. For that reason, she was not a particular fan of spelling exercises, except when it came to general rules. As she put it, "If you have good visual memory, you can spell. If you don't, you can't."

When each new delegation of kids arrived at his house, Seamus was supposed to have them review the work he'd completed that had been brought by his previous visitors.

This imposed a purpose and rhythm to the visits. Elaine knew it would be acceptable, under the circumstances, for the kids to just show up and amuse themselves with Seamus. But it wouldn't be the same.

"Did you do your work?" asked AJ. The kids were on good behavior, so no one joked about the fact that AJ, not the most diligent of students, was the one to question Seamus.

Seamus beamed. He'd done it. It was there on the coffee table, two work sheets with careful pencil markings. Until now, Seamus had been the sort of boy who was too much on the go to give full attention to the mechanics of penmanship. His handwriting had improved with illness.

Alex, Jake, AJ, and Danielle surrounded Seamus. Alex wore a friendship bracelet that she and Seamus had made during a crafts project in the fall. It was woven from four strips of colored yarn. Her friends Michelle and Laura had teased her that Seamus had a crush on her and the accusation had made her blush.

The homework sheets lay between them in the middle of the table. Today's involved math. Elaine had given the kids some "manipulatives" consisting of pattern blocks to use in demonstrating fractions for Seamus. Manipulatives, Elaine had found, were especially popular with boys, and pattern blocks were exactly the sort of educational tool that a family wasn't likely to have around the house.

Generally, Seamus was working on lessons a few days after the class had done the same assignment. It was possible for the children to correct his work with something approaching teacherlike assurance. If there was uncertainty, Susan Farrell or the parent-chauffeur were consulted. The kids then brought Seamus's work back to school for Elaine to review. He still craved feedback from Mrs. Moore.

Susan would try to give the kids their own space. This was Seamus's time with his friends, and it was important that it be his world, on his terms, with minimal intrusion from her. School had been that way for him and she sensed it was that feeling of inhabiting a world that was friendly and familiar, a world in which he felt something like an ownership stake, a world that was *his*, that he missed most about Ravenwood.

It was remarkable how serious the kids were. They hunched over each of Seamus's work sheets with the determined concentration of private tutors entrusted with the tutelage of a young prince who would someday need to rule wisely over vast territories. They complimented Seamus on his correct answers and patiently explained what had gone wrong with the others. There was something impressively tunnel-visioned about their approach. They really wanted him to get it right, to learn what *they* were learning, and presumably for the very same reasons. As Mrs. Moore had explained at the very start of the school year, learning was something we do our entire life. It is what makes us who we are. If we stop learning, we call that . . .

One time Susan overhead a little girl crouched beside Seamus at the coffee table tell him, in the gently scolding tones a teacher might use, "You know, when you grow up, you're going to need to know this stuff."

• • •

The visits to Seamus's house were segmented roughly into thirds: during the first third, the kids ate lunch and bantered as if they were in the Ravenwood cafeteria; then came schoolwork, as the kids corrected the work Seamus had done and explained new assignments being passed on to him, just as Mrs. Moore would do; then came free time. Depending on Seamus's energy level, this involved toy-car racing, reading comic books like *Spawn* or *Spiderman,* or listening to music. Jim's state police colleague Lee Farmer, a rock-and-roll drummer in his prelaw-enforcement years, had given Seamus several Def Leppard CDs.

Seamus was invariably in high spirits for these visits. He kidded and laughed in a way that Susan rarely saw him do at other times. He could joke with his classmates in a way that gave him the special comfort he sought, the reassurance that he was still part of their circle.

He was, to a degree, a horror to look at. Adults who saw him frequently had to look away. Not the kids. More than once he referred to himself as getting close to "kicking the bucket." It was said matter-of-factly. The kids knew what he meant, and did not flinch.

On this day, Seamus motioned for them to move to his bedroom, which adjoined the living room.

They got up and followed him in.

It was a small room with one single bed for him and a bunk bed that had belonged to Colin and Jesse. The room was crammed with boyhood paraphernalia, a bolt-action squirt gun, a stack of *Predators,* a deflated soccer ball, a framed photo of him hoisting a fish he'd caught at Quartz Creek, a shelf piled with his expanding collection of caps: NYPD, Navy Seal Team, U.S. Air Force, LAPD, Seagraves Fire Co. There was a glass terrarium, given to him by Joseph and his girlfriend, containing two sprightly anole lizards. They were green and small with pads on their feet and Seamus named them Bix and Nimbus after characters in *Dinotopia.* The bedroom's one window looked out on the white expanse of the backyard.

Seamus motioned for the kids to make themselves comfortable, on his bed or Colin's.

"What's up?" asked Jake.

The children glanced around his room. There was a lot of stuff, but it was mostly familiar stuff, Seuss books and monster posters. Their own rooms were like this. And why not? Seamus was just a regular kid. A regular fun kid with a good heart and a big smile who accepted others without judgment. That's who he was. That, and the awful tumor. In fact, spending a lunchtime like this with him, joking and jabbering, it was easy to think of him as nothing but a fellow student in Mrs. Moore's fourth-grade class, a member of their circle, a ten-year-old who liked pretty much the same things they liked and valued most of what they valued and viewed the big mountainous world and the deep valleys carving through it and the infinite sky above with the same mix of bewilderment and awe—and yes, sometimes boredom—that they did. The kids waited for Seamus to come to his point.

"What do you think heaven's like?" He finally asked, with eagerness and sincerity. "Do you think there'll be pets in heaven?"

The kids were caught by surprise. It wasn't a subject to which they'd given a lot of consideration.

"Problem is, I can't really talk to Mom and Dad about this," Seamus explained. "They're not ready yet."

· 6 ·

UPON A STAR

The sun rose earlier these days and lingered until dinnertime. Children waiting for the morning bus were at last able to see each other's faces without the illumination of passing headlights. To be sure, the elements of winter were still present, with slushy roads still walled by tall piles of snow and the outdoor ice rinks still glistening. But it was March now and, even in Alaska, one had the sense that deepest winter had passed. And Seamus Farrell was still alive.

Six weeks had been the doctor's prognosis back in late December, and that was meant to be conservative. Of course, there was a margin of error, give or take some weeks, as was always the case in statistical estimates.

Susan and Jim Farrell knew better than to get their hopes up. Their son had lived longer than predicted. That was a blessing and they dared not contemplate anything beyond that.

In his good moments, he was a version of the same old Seamus. He no longer wrestled or built snow forts with Jesse and Colin. He had little strength and no mobility. But the boys did play board games. They watched sports on TV. They talked and laughed and argued. They didn't stop being brothers. A few taunts were thrown, as well as an occasional solid object. The brief interludes that felt like old times were small miracles. Susan read to the twins, as she'd been doing since they were toddlers. There were times when Jim came home and, if his day with the troopers had not been too grim, told funny stories of people he'd met. It still thrilled Jim to be peppered by Seamus with observations—on football, the weather, monsters, you name it—in the same eager way he always had, gazing up with his twinkling eyes to ask, "Right, Dad?"

That phrase—so earnest, so curious, so instinctual—signified their relationship. It was pure Seamus. "Right, Dad?"

Around this time, the Farrells learned about the Make-A-Wish Foundation, a national nonprofit agency with affiliates in each state whose mission is "granting a wish" of young children who are suffering from life-threatening medical conditions. Eligibility requirements are specific and blunt: the child has to be older than two and a half years and younger than eighteen, and the essential hopelessness of the child's prognosis has to be verified by a physician. The foundation relies on a referral system for discovering candidates. The referrals can come directly from the child, from the child's parents or guardian, or from a professional treating the child, such as a social worker, nurse, or doctor.

In Seamus's case, the referral came through Ron Rice, an Anchorage police officer who learned about Seamus through one of Jim's trooper colleagues. Rice was an executive with the Wish Upon the North Star foundation, affiliated with Make-A-Wish.

Economically speaking, the Farrells were of middle-class means. They owned their home on a half-acre lot. Jim's job earned him a salary adequate to maintaining the family in a comfortable lifestyle. Frills, such as they were, amounted to toys for the kids, camping trips to spectacular places in their pop-up tent, and a visit every few years to relatives in the east. The boys had plenty of clothes and outdoor gear, although hand-me-downs from Jesse were certainly part of Seamus and Colin's wardrobe. What they lacked, as with so many middle-class families, was a margin of savings sufficient to cover catastrophic illness.

Yes, they had insurance that covered family medical needs, including Seamus's surgery, hospitalization, and follow-up treatments. When not tending to Seamus's immediate needs, and those of Colin and Jesse, Susan gathered a mountain of information about his tumor, desperately seeking second opinions and alternative perspectives. Her return to nursing school was on hold, but her immersion in the world of medical information could not be more determined. Emotionally, it was an almost impossibly difficult high-wire act, to begin making "peace" with Seamus's impending death while expending maximum effort to explore what else, if anything, might be done.

Susan had copies of Seamus's CAT scans sent to Children's Hospital in Seattle, where there were doctors who specialized in brain tumors. She also sent the scans to doctors at the University of California–San Francisco Medical Center. This was in the pre-Internet era. She made contact with these institutions through phone calls and anxiously waited to learn their findings by means of return calls and regular mail. In both instances, the urban medical centers— with a depth of expertise beyond what was available locally in Anchorage—confirmed her fears. The Providence Medical Center doctors were correct. Nothing could be done.

Still, they explored every halfway plausible lead. A neighbor of Susan's happened to see an episode of *The Oprah Winfrey Show* featuring a New York doctor who specialized in treating children with difficult cancers and who, fortified by the bold claim that he "would not let them die," was meeting with some success. The next day, Jim telephoned the show's studio in Chicago and managed to speak with a producer who gave him the doctor's phone number. Jim called and the doctor agreed to review Seamus's CAT scans. Jim and Susan waited with guarded hope. But the doctor, they soon learned, had no suggestions. There was nothing he could do.

The appeal to Wish Upon the North Star and Make-A-Wish represented a further acknowledgement that, while continuing to aggressively investigate all conceivable options, the time had arrived to circle their wagons and invest what remained of their energies and spirit in providing Seamus with as much happiness as possible in the time he had left.

Once a child is approved for Make-A-Wish, the foundation assigns a volunteer "wish team" to coordinate the wish-granting process. Volunteers begin by asking a simple question: "If you could have one wish, what would it be?"

Most wishes, according to the foundation, fall into one of four categories: "I want to go to . . ."; "I want to be . . ."; "I want to meet . . ."; or "I want to have . . ."

Make-A-Wish children get to meet entertainment stars they idolize. They get to attend the Superbowl or lace up skates and cruise the ice with their favorite hockey team. The most obvious wish, of course, cannot be mentioned. Or granted.

Seamus's wish was to go to Disney World with his parents and brothers. He'd heard stories about it from an Eagle River boy who'd been there and of course he'd seen more than a few commercials touting the glorious fun that was all but guaranteed. Disney World had rides. It had theme parks. There were live stage performances, a Tower of Terror, the Magic Kingdom, the Epcot Center; and the weather was rumored to be perpetual summer.

The Farrells were notified that Seamus's wish had been granted, and they prepared to go as soon as possible.

When Seamus's upcoming trip to Florida was mentioned in class, everyone was happy for him. Alex Vanderhoff went straight home the day she learned about it and told her mother. Her mother immediately burst into tears.

Alex was confused by her mother's response, since Disney World was supposed to be such a fantastic place to visit.

This wonderful trip, her mom was forced to explain, was only presented to children who were not expected to live much longer.

• • •

In March, the theme in Elaine's classroom was "Accepting Challenges." Facing up to difficult situations, and striving to overcome them, was a core lesson any teacher would want to impart. In Eagle River, the concept tied in neatly with the annual running of the Iditarod, the grueling dogsled race across jagged mountain ranges and desolate tundra from Anchorage all the way up to Nome on the Bering Sea.

Billed as "The Last Great Race on Earth," it is a competition like no other. The Iditarod was named after a gold-rush town, abandoned long ago, that lay on a mail and supply route connecting the Pacific coast to the Alaskan interior. Mail and supplies went in, and gold came out. All by means of dogsled.

The trail gained renown in 1925 when Nome was

endangered by a diphtheria epidemic. The nearest life-saving serum was in Anchorage, a distance of 1,049 miles through thick, mountainous wilderness. The Alaska Railroad was able to ferry the medicine about 250 miles north. From there, volunteer dogsled drivers relayed the serum the rest of the way. Temperatures en route were sometimes fifty degrees below zero. It was literally a race against death. According to legend, the serum was nearly lost when a blast of arctic wind toppled the sled of the final musher. Frantically, he dug through the snow with his bare hands to retrieve it. Nome was saved.

The Iditarod and the lore surrounding it are ripe with opportunities for teaching, especially to someone like Elaine. Geography, reading (she challenged the students to read for 1,049 extra minutes during the month), Native American culture, nature, science, math, writing (she asked them to try writing from the point of view of the lead dog), and art, to name a few, could all be integrated into an appreciation of the Iditarod. Plus, Eagle River is the first checkpoint on the race route, and nearly everyone in town turns out to cheer on the mushers.

Elaine's students got to select a musher (of the sixty or so teams that entered) and follow his or her progress through the daily reports in the news. That year there were several entrants of special note. Susan Butcher, the first woman to win the race (in 1986), was racing for what might be her last time. Jeff King, an up-and-comer noted for his innovative and "humanitarian" treatment of his dogs, was another to watch. There were teams from several countries. In truth, all the mushers had interesting stories, for they all shared an exceptional quality: they had actively undertaken an extremely difficult challenge.

Elaine would tell the kids about the incredible preparation (hundreds of hours and thousands of miles spent in training the dogs, training themselves) it took to compete. She regaled them with accounts of the inhospitable terrain and the horrifically inclement weather the teams confronted. Windchill temperatures could be 100 degrees below zero, Fahrenheit. Violent storms could strand mushers or, if they lost the trail, force them to painstakingly backtrack. Rampaging moose could destroy equipment or injure dogs. And the mushers, driven to win, rarely rested, averaging about two hours sleep per night during the race.

"Why would someone put up with all that?" she asked.

"It's cool."

"There are easier ways to do something cool," she responded.

"You get money."

Elaine stood there without commenting, for ten seconds, then twenty, silently scanning the group. Everyone understood this to mean that she did not accept this explanation.

"It's not that much money," she told them. "Anyway, would you do all that just on a longshot chance you might get some prize money?" The kids looked at each other. They were young enough not to have a firm appreciation of exactly what $50,000 in prize money meant. They did, however, have a vague sense of what it might mean to spend approximately two weeks, night and day, in below-zero weather skidding through the Alaskan wilderness. On second thought, they were prepared to accept that money might not be the primary motivation for Iditarod mushers.

"Maybe," offered one girl, remembering this month's theme, "they just like the challenge of it?"

Yes! The mushers liked the challenge of it!

"What part of the challenge do you think they like?" Elaine asked.

"How hard it is."

"Adventure."

"Getting dogs to obey."

"Just seeing if they can make it to Nome."

"Do any of you," Elaine asked, "have challenges in your life that are difficult and not always fun but you want to try anyway?"

"Seamus does," someone answered.

The children were silent. There was no need for Elaine to point out the distinction. She could see on their faces that it registered: as challenges go, the Iditarod was a stroll in the park compared to what Seamus faced.

• • •

Escaping late-winter Alaska for the semitropical splendor of Disney World seemed to the Farrells to be almost in itself a dream. Instead of padded coats and thermal hats, people ambled around unhurriedly in loose T-shirts and baggy shorts. Even coming through the airport terminal at Orlando, they had the feeling of coming to a place where everyday worries had been left behind and vacation reigned.

By this time, Seamus could move about only in a wheelchair. Because the steroids he'd been taking to ease the painful swelling in his skull had produced a voracious appetite, Seamus now weighed more than double what he'd weighed only a few months before. He had a nearly insatiable desire for Taco Bell, sometimes racing his weight-lifting brother Joseph to see who could polish off a box of six soft tacos the fastest.

Susan and Jim had no interest in steering him to healthier food or curbing his desires. Giving him what he wanted was, indeed, exactly what they wanted. That alone—not what was good for him in the impossible long term, not a balanced selection of the four essential food groups—was what mattered. This stage had but one clear, easy-to-identify objective: let Seamus smile as much as possible.

In Disney World, they'd come to the right place.

They got VIP treatment all the way. A van with wheelchair capacity had been rented for them. They would be staying in a luxury three-bedroom suite at Kids Village in Kissimmee. They would be provided special passes for circumventing the famously long lines at many rides and exhibits. If Seamus needed physical assistance in climbing into a roller-coaster car or gaining access to any part of the park, a Disney employee would be at the ready to help out.

Food and beverages were free. All tickets to all events were free. The van was free. The airfare was free. The accommodations were free. When Seamus was especially thrilled by some activity—as he was, for example, by the ride through Magic Mountain—he needed only to mention it to a Disney tour guide and—whoosh!—he was escorted back on again, ahead of the line.

Inevitably, there were sobering moments. Touring Epcot Center's pavilions—Universe of Energy, The Living Seas, Spaceship Earth—Seamus turned to Jim, who was merrily pushing him through this cornucopia of amazements, and said, "I'm not going to get to see this—the future. Right, Dad?"

But for the most part, it was five action-packed, nonstop, high-voltage, Technicolor, surround-sound, fun-all-the-time-in-every-way days and nights. It was the absolute, consummate, total-immersion family enjoyment experience under Kodak-moment conditions: children and parents together, pampered and buoyed, free from work, free from schedules, free from obligations, free from annoyances, free at last to indulge in the single thing the Farrells most wished for—enjoying each other's company.

For Joseph, who was older, wiser, and more worldly than his brothers—which is to say far less of a child—there was a bittersweet undercurrent, camouflaged by the frenetic mirth and balmy weather. "I'd step back sometimes and see my parents, and they were so happy, just laughing and laughing," Joseph recalled. "And it seemed like they'd entered the fantasy world, too."

The Magic Kingdom fireworks display was the culmination of a parade, termed the Electric Light Parade, along the fabled Main Street re-creation—actually, more like a fantasy idealization—of a simpler, kinder, slower, chummier small-town America, where neighbors knew neighbors (and liked them) and shopkeepers knew shoppers (and didn't fleece them), and the calendar year was laced with civic events where the whole town gathered together and was delighted.

The Farrells were able to secure a spot along the Main Street curb with a view unobstructed by trees or people. The display was set for the sky directly above Cinderella's Castle. Jim, Susan, Colin, Jesse, and Joseph, with Seamus in the middle, craned their necks and waited. From the window flew the famous orb of dancing light. Tinkerbell fluttered her trademark zigzag flutter, higher, higher, up to the castle's peak. Then the show began.

A warm night sky. Stillness, silence, anticipation. Then the sharp crackling report as though from a sniper's gun. Then another, and another. The night exploded in brilliant patterns of light—yellows, greens, silvers, purples, and golds, flashdancing across the black-satin backdrop.

Fireworks are, of course, more than just a dazzling visual treat. They fill your chest, your heart, your lungs, your mind. Seeing the night burst with exploding bouquets of light is to imagine, if fleetingly, that any night, any darkness, can magically brighten. A night of shooting lights is a night unlike others. Anything, it seems, is possible.

Throughout their stay, the Farrells encountered a classic

Disney theme song, possibly *the* classic song. Muted, like a subconscious yearning, the tune played in the background at the hotel elevators and amusement park rides, at ticket kiosks and hidden speakers at restaurant booths. That song marked the thrilling culmination of the fireworks.

When you wish upon a star,
makes no difference who you are
Anything your heart desires will come to you

If your heart is in your dreams, no request is too extreme
When you wish upon a star as dreamers do

Like a bolt out of the blue, fate steps in and sees you through
When you wish upon a star, your dreams come true

In the midst of this tumultuous spectacle of fantastic light, Colin fell apart. The chaos, or the manufactured atmosphere of chaos, got to him. In the complicated mechanisms of his mind, a switch was thrown.

"Turn it off! I want it turned off!" He jammed his finger in his ears, shut his eyes, and hollered for the pyrotechnics to stop.

Colin's inner world was largely an enigma. The pain he endured by being different from others could only be guessed at. For whatever reason, the Magic Kingdom fireworks display, that crafted crown jewel to the quintessential perfect kid's day, was driving him crazy. He wanted the noise, the night, the lights to stop!

Seamus, who protected Colin against all taunts and abuse, who was almost as attached to Colin as he was to his own limbs, turned to his twin and for the first time anyone could remember, snapped, "Colin, be quiet!"

Susan hustled Colin into the nearest curio shop, the old-timey general store with its swinging screen door and quaint wooden shelves stocked with nineteenth-century dry goods (as well as contemporary soft drinks and snacks).

Back on Main Street, the fireworks built rhythmically, ineluctably toward a dizzying crescendo of color and light and noise. Upturned faces shimmered and glowed.

Seamus was ecstatic. "I can't believe I'm actually here!" he exclaimed over and over. "I just can't believe I'm really here! I can't believe I'm here."

And then it was over.

• • •

In the northern zones, the stretch of time just before the full onset of spring is often a good one for teachers. They know the kids well by now and the children, too, have found their groove. The panic that comes from not knowing whether it will be possible to squeeze in the entire load of basic curriculum material by year's end has somewhat subsided. The finish line might still be out of sight, but there is a confidence that the pace they've established, bit by bit, day by day, week by week, will get them there.

In Room 112, life went on.

Back from Disney World, Seamus's condition began to deteriorate. He was vomiting a lot again, and the home health nurse, Pat Burry, became a fixture in their household.

Seamus still craved the visits from his classmates, but it was obvious to the students that he was far weaker than he'd been even a month before, and that the energy and concentration required for schoolwork was often more than he could summon. One time when the group arrived, Seamus met them without a hat on, which was a shock to Susan. Usually he took such effort to conceal his scarred and patchy scalp. And he took such pride in his array of insignia hats, making it a point to wear a different one for each visit. Greeting his classmates bareheaded struck Susan almost as a sign of surrender.

The kids, happily, skipped right on in and spread out for lunch without acknowledgment or comment. It was weird. They did not look at him with pity. Indeed, what was perhaps pitiful in his appearance—his bloated body and puffy face, his ruined hair, his immobility—seemed almost invisible to them. They walked through the door and said "hi." They looked him in the eye. They asked if he wanted to share their corn chips. They did not dwell on his infirmity. What they saw was a friend on the edge of death who was the same boy they'd tussled with on the playground and bantered with in class. What they saw was his original self.

"These kids were aware of death every time they went over there," observed Joan Johnson. "They were aware that this little boy might die. They saw how puffed up he was with the steroids that were being given to him and they didn't care. They saw a classmate going through death and they wanted to be there for him, and with him. They could go over there and be with him and give him some kind of life. It gave them a sense of what you do with someone who is dying: you help them in any way you can. You make their life good before death takes them. What better way of showing kids how to do that? You can't read about it. You do it."

• • •

There were times when Seamus was not able to complete the lessons. With little or nothing of his work to go over or correct, the kids would read to him instead from a book that Elaine was reading to the class, Brian Jacques's *Redwall*.

The operating budget for Alaska public schools roughly follows the boom-or-bust fluctuations in the state economy. When the oil flows, so do the funds into the school-district budget. When oil and gas prices are high, when military spending is peaking, Alaska is in the chips. And the schools with funding from a state legislature suddenly awash in revenues are a direct beneficiary. As a consequence, not only are teacher salaries decent—make that "adequate"—but there is money available for an array of special projects that in more frugal times would be considered unthinkable.

School visits by established authors are one such item, and earlier that year Ravenwood had been able to secure a date for the acclaimed British children's book author Brian Jacques to visit. Author of the *Redwall* series, once described by an insensitive adult as a "gothic rodent epic," Jacques is a master storyteller with a big-hearted appreciation for the concerns of children old enough to heed the moral complexities of the world they inhabit. Like Tolkien, Jacques's world is delightfully make-believe, laced with stark conflicts between good and evil that strike young readers as searingly real.

"Cluny was a bilge rat; the biggest, most savage rodent that ever jumped from ship to shore," went a passage from *Redwall,* which Jacques had introduced to the Ravenwood kids. "He was black, with grey and pink scars all over his huge sleek body, from the tip of his wet nose, up past his green and yellow slitted eye, across both his mean tattered ears, down the length of his heavy vermin-ridden back to the enormous whiplike tail which had earned him his title: Cluny the Scourge!"

Elaine kept a quote from Jacques's presentation on the message board so the kids would see it every time they lined up at the door: "Grow up brave and honest like a real Redwaller, kind to your family and true to your friends."

● ● ●

Elaine had been considering the idea of the class making a quilt for Seamus. Back in February, as part of the Black History Month program, Elaine had read the class an illustrated book titled *Sweet Clara and the Freedom Quilt*. The book told the story of a young slave girl in the Civil War–era South who learned the craft of patching together a quilt and also learned how the needlework on the patches can covertly convey secret information. In the book, this turned out to be a map of the hidden routes of the Underground Railroad by which slaves might escape to freedom.

"I worked on the quilt for a long time," Clara tells us. "Sometimes months would go by and I wouldn't get any pieces sewn in it. Sometimes I had to wait to get the right kind of cloth—I had blue calico and flowered blue silk for creeks and rivers, and greens and blue-greens for the fields, and white sheeting for roads."

In discussing the book, Elaine would tell the kids about her own encounters with the lingering effects of segregation—how she'd watched her father's baseball team play a touring team of great Negro League stars who came north to play in Manitoba because blacks were not allowed in the major leagues. Or the time she spent in Columbus, Georgia, in 1964 when her husband was attached to Fort Benning. Blacks there stepped off the sidewalks when white people approached. The public hospital had separate waiting rooms for the races. Elaine was pregnant then with her first daughter and briefly made a protest, stating that she would not consider going to a doctor's office that was segregated. "Well, good luck, honey," she was told. "That's the only kind we have."

Elaine first became familiar with quilts through her former mother-in-law, who'd been raised in the Appalachian region of West Virginia and owned several heirloom quilts that conveyed aspects of family history, with exquisitely embroidered dates of birth and death. She knew that quilts held a special place in the world of crafts and cultural history.

"Quilts touch our deepest longings for ourselves and our children, opening direct channels to our emotions, hopes, and dreams as only great art can," wrote Robert Shaw in *Quilts: A Living Tradition*. "They are the most intimate of objects, created out of love and care, metaphorically wrapping the sleeper in the warmth and concern of the maker's affection, promising comfort, protection, and peace through the night's dark uncertainties."

Of course! The class should make Seamus a quilt.

It made perfect sense. A quilt, if you thought about it, was an analogue for so much of what the class was doing, and so much of Elaine's teaching.

As an educator, Elaine valued the notion of "part to whole" learning, which theorized that subject areas, from reading to math, can be mastered piece by piece and later synthesized into a "whole" understanding. "Parts" were not merely incomplete or insufficient elements; they had their own integrity.

Part to whole. Each part existed in the context of the whole, yet the whole was dependent on its parts. The whole derives its form, its shape, its meaning, its character, its identity, its very soul, from the assemblage of its component parts. Change a part, and the whole is transfigured. Master a part and the whole might be within your grasp. Part to whole. Lesson plans were patches to understanding the whole. Time was a blanket, and each day a square.

Although not herself a quilter, Elaine knew she could rely on some of the parents to help. Seamus's plight and the kids' concern for him was, by now, an ongoing topic in every Room 112 household. It was discussed at night at dinner, on the weekends at home, in the aisles at Carrs grocery store when parents ran into each other, even in the pages of the *Chugiak–Eagle River Star*, which ran an article about their visits, headlined "Friends help youth battle brain tumor."

At Circle Time, Elaine floated the idea of making a quilt for Seamus. What, she asked, should it look like?

It was agreed that the quilt could be all different colors.

But it could not be all different shapes. Squares were the necessary building blocks. Everyone knew about building blocks.

How many squares? Well, that was sort of a math problem. A division problem, really.

The students formed a committee to plan the quilt. Elaine strongly encouraged cooperative groups, and this seemed a project tailor-made for such a process. Details remained to be sorted out. But something was clear: pieces were slipping into their slots with a precision you normally find only in math solutions. Yes, a quilt designed to comfort Seamus promised the simple elegance of a mathematical proof.

Gradually, the quilt idea was refined. Each child,

including Seamus, would be responsible for the artwork on one square. The final squares would be a collective effort and reflect a collective theme.

Getting Seamus to create his own square presented a problem, since an added dimension of the project, about which all the kids were quite adamant, was to present the quilt to him as a surprise. As happens with kids, they had already projected ahead in their plans to the awesome celebration that would take place upon presenting it to him, as a surprise, on a visit to Ravenwood when the weather was warmer and he felt a little better. That would be so wonderful. Just to see his face as they handed it to him.

But first they had to make it.

• • •

Elaine strongly encouraged parent participation in the classroom, and would send a note home at the start of each school year asking parents what skills they had to offer and what contributions they'd like to make. By this time in the school year, the parents were almost like a veteran hockey team, where each player knew his teammates' strengths. "We all knew what each other's talents were," said Kay Pederson, a rosy-cheeked, round-faced, ultracapable blonde woman.

Kay had bona fide quilting experience. She was the current Ravenwood PTA president, the mother of six, and an army wife whose husband was posted in remote Bethel, Alaska, a quasi-civilized outpost four hundred miles to the east. Kay also ran a home day care service before and after school five days a week. She was, in brief, very busy. But she agreed to be responsible for sewing the kids' squares onto a suitable backing to make the quilt.

Barbara Bernard, a self-described "craft-impaired" person, helped out by obtaining the muslin squares from an Anchorage fabric store, along with the special crayons the kids would need to create individualized patches. On the appointed day, each child was given special crayons and special art paper the same size as the fabric squares.

Elaine's instruction to the children was minimal and to the point.

"This is for Seamus. What you draw is up to you. It can be a favorite thing to you, or a memory of something special. It's up to you. Quilts are really pieces of memory. But it should be a picture that will help Seamus know that it's from you."

"Can't we just put our name on it?"

"No, because it will iron on backwards."

"Oh, yeah."

Elaine told them that after they were done with their drawing, they were to write a note to Seamus, telling him about it. The note plus the original drawing, she said, were going to be assembled in an album that they would give to him along with the finished quilt.

The kids drew carefully on the squares of drawing paper. It was hard for Elaine to guess what they would do. Her kids were used to assignments—if that's what you wanted to call this—that were open-ended. Like: If you could be any animal, which one would you choose to be and why? Or: If today could be a holiday celebrating something you loved, what would the holiday be and what would you do on this day? Blank pieces of paper to be filled with expressive writing and blank muslin squares to be filled with colorful drawings were not, to Elaine's kids, the daunting, insurmountable cliffs they might be to schoolchildren accustomed to more right-answer, wrong-answer types of instruction.

Elaine knew the quilt must be completed soon. She'd heard Seamus was faltering. *Borrowed time,* a common phrase tossed casually into daily conversation, held something close to a literal meaning in this situation. Another common word, *deadline,* was much on Elaine's mind.

The kids scrunched over their desks. Elaine strolled among them, looking over their shoulders, smiling, nodding. Room 112 was quiet. The only sounds were background sounds: crayons clicking against paper, antsy feet knocking against desk legs, the overhead hum of fluorescent lights, a cough, a sniffle, a self-satisfied sigh. This was the quiet of a church, the quiet of a library, the quiet of a laboratory, the deep quiet of a writer's studio.

As each child finished, his or her square was handed to one of the parents who'd come to help. An ironing board was set up and the drawings were pressed onto the twelve-inch muslin squares that would make up the quilt.

It was a magical moment, an unveiling punctuated by

"oohs" and "aahs." The drawing paper lifted, and there it was, their very own artwork transferred with a kind of permanence to fabric. Soon to be a quilt! The heat of the iron had intensified the colors. The blues were deeper, the reds more vivid. The greens of the grass and trees felt alive and soothing. The yellow of the sun seemed to give off warmth.

"Oooh."

"Wow."

Michelle Foss drew a wide strip of blue pouring across brown boulders, with the sun above and swirling water below. "I did a waterfall because waterfalls are peaceful. And I want you to feel peaceful, too," she wrote in careful print across the lined paper.

Logan Tucker, a blond boy with big eyes, drew a smiling warrior in yellow breastplate standing on a grassy cliff raising his sword to do battle with a fire-breathing dragon. "My quilt square of a knight fighting a dragon represents me because I love fantasy," he wrote. "I really enjoyed making this for you because I got a chance to draw on paper in school and another reason I liked making it was I was making it for someone special."

Sarah Chapman drew the sky bright orange. Her sun was shaped like a Valentine's heart. A rainbow arched across the landscape. She wrote, "I did my quilt square of a rainbow because everyone needs a rainbow and a little sunshine after the storm."

Feisty AJ Pederson drew a rocket ship composed of little

orange bricks shooting across the night, with a creature in a helmet at the controls. "The reason I did Legos," he wrote, "is because I'm crazy about Legos and you know that too so once you see the quilt you'd know what square was mine."

Moving from group to group, peeking here and there like a proctor at an exam, it was hard for Elaine not to burst into cheers. The artwork was exceptional, made with a thoughtfulness and attention to elements like perspective and layout that struck her as far beyond what they'd previously demonstrated. Were they old enough to actually get "inspired" in the way that term was used concerning artists and the dream-state in which they produced their best work? Were the kids mature enough to actually be touched by the muse? Was there an age eligibility for that? And could the famously elusive muse visit an entire class, all together and all at once? That seemed to her to be what was happening.

And not just the artwork, but the accompanying notes. Some, yes, were your basic fourth-grade minimalism. But others were strange, deep, complex, cryptic.

Mild-mannered Daniel Lee wrote, "My quilt square is about running through the woods at night when there is hardly any light. A little guy who's not very shy goes pitter patting beside me making as least noise as possible. I look down and smile and he smiles back. I go inside to get some breakfast. Then I offer some to him and he takes it and puts it in his store and comes begging for more. I say wait till another day." The drawing was a close-up of two bare legs extending from knobby knees to bow-tied gym shoes, standing in a cone of light with darkness all around. A shy squirrel peeked out from behind the ankles.

Cheerful Michelle Moore drew an orange cat with a green neck ribbon poised atop a piece of furniture. Will it leap or simply continue to stare? "I made a cat because cats are soft and cuddly," she wrote. "Now every time you are feeling lonely just cuddle up with our quilt and it will make you feel better."

"We will never forget you Seamus because you are special and unique to our classroom," wrote David Schwartz. "My picture represents our love for you. The bright blue sky and the beautiful green birch trees."

"My quilt square is a dragon for that is my favorite thing on earth," wrote Erik Johnson in a heavy script suggesting great earnestness, no irony intended. "I want you to know that I pray for you every day. I love you Seamus and I swear it with my own blood."

A square was still needed from Seamus. Obtaining it turned out to require less subterfuge than anticipated. On their next visit to his house, the kids simply brought a square of paper and the special crayons and asked him to draw a picture of something that he really liked. The kids told him it was to be part of something the class was preparing to give Mrs. Moore to thank her for being such a neat teacher.

Seamus looked at the blank page.

"Everyone's doing this?"

The kids nodded.

"Anything I want?"

"Anything."

"What did other kids draw?"

"A horse."

"A dragon."

"A soccer ball."

He picked up a blue crayon and began filling in the entire square. Ocean? Sky?

In the top left corner, he drew an object jutting downward. Rocket ship? Monster's claw?

The kids watching him do this were perplexed. Based on his well-known affection for aliens, they could venture a guess. But it had none of the easy reference points, no pointy head, no Cyclops eye, no glowing disc spinning among distant stars.

They waited for him to explain.

"Do you like it?" he asked.

They knew what Mrs. Moore would say. "Sure, Seamus. It's you."

Kay Pederson took the squares home and began the process of assembling them into a finished quilt. For the sashing that would unite the squares, Kay found a black fabric speckled with red, yellow, blue, and green letters of the alphabet strewn throughout the fabric at jumbled angles as though they'd been flung onto it. Using yarn, Kay tied the squares, usually at the corners, to the alphabet fabric. It was slow work. Each time she picked up a square and tried to determine where in the pattern to place it, she couldn't help reflecting on why this was being done. "This isn't like making a baby quilt," Kay thought to herself. "This isn't to welcome a child into the world. This could be what they bury him in."

She worried she might not finish before Seamus passed away.

When it was done a few days later, Kay returned the quilt to Room 112. It was unveiled at Circle Time to a chorus of "wows." It was carefully hung across the rear of the classroom, in a space always reserved for their artwork.

These were sunny days now in Eagle River, a long way from December. Daylight lasted for over seventeen hours a day, and counting. The room was bright and the kids were proud of the quilt they'd made for Seamus. It hung on the wall where they could gaze at it whenever they wanted. Alex was exceedingly proud to see that her careful drawing of a cat appeared at the top center of the finished quilt.

The kids began planning the party. Seamus would come to Ravenwood and they'd surprise him with the quilt, along with the letters they'd written. Maybe they'd read their letters aloud while he sat in his wheelchair and listened. They knew how happy that would make him, how he'd laugh at the little in-jokes (about Legos and *Redwall*) and be moved by their notes. It would surely be a Celebration Day, marking the date in early May when the air outside was soft and sweet. Seamus Receives His Quilt Day.

Elaine checked with Susan Farrell. Friday, Susan thought, would work fine. He couldn't stay long, Susan cautioned. But she was sure it would give him a boost.

On Friday morning, Elaine received a message from the school secretary that Seamus wasn't feeling up to the visit. Susan suggested Monday instead.

The kids were disappointed, but they could wait until Seamus was well enough for the celebration.

On Monday, Seamus was still too weak to make the trip. He'd been asleep much of the past couple of days and was showing little enthusiasm, even for visiting Ravenwood. Again, Elaine explained to the kids that the celebration would need to be postponed.

So the quilt hung there, waiting for Seamus.

On their way out for recess or lunch or gym or to the library, the kids could admire it, and themselves for having made it. It really was something to behold. It measured six by seven feet. The black sashing strewn with alphabet letters vividly framed the brightly colored squares. To round out the number of squares to a perfectly geometrical thirty, four others had been created, one for each corner: a black raven winging across a yellow sun with the words RAVENWOOD ELEMENTARY; red lettering on a white patch: MRS. MOORE'S 4TH GRADE; another square with lettering, MADE IN LOVING COLOR, ROOM 112; and finally, in the lower right corner, an open book. GOOD BOOKS, Elaine had written across the open pages, GOOD FRIENDS.

• • •

Elaine was at home a few nights later. The phone rang and it was Susan Farrell. Seamus had sunk into a coma and was dying. A minister was at the house and the end was near. Could she please come?

"I'll be right over."

Elaine threw on her coat. The Farrells lived only a couple of miles away. She could be there in minutes.

Elaine arrived to find the scene she'd dreaded. Seamus was in bed in his bedroom, comatose. Susan and Jim were at his side. A priest or minister was there, and everyone was bowed in prayer. It resembled a scene of last rites.

Then it struck her: the quilt! The class had never had the chance to give Seamus the beautiful quilt.

She abruptly left and raced to Ravenwood, a short drive. It was nearly 10 PM She knew the school would be closed at that hour, but hoped she could find the custodian.

When she arrived, the school was locked. No yellow buses in the traffic circle, no curbside gaggle of kids and grown-ups, no signs of life anywhere in this place usually teeming with life.

Elaine parked her car right in front, and ran to the double glass doors. Some lights were still on. Was that always the case after hours? She could not recall. She peered in but saw no movement. She pounded on the door and window, pounded with as much force as she felt the glass could with-stand. Nothing.

Elaine started running around the edge of the school, moving window to window along the straightaway toward her room, pounding, making noise, calling out, trying to rouse the custodian.

The interiors of the classrooms appeared so different from this vantage point, the vantage point of a person desperately trying to gain entrance. Each room was a miniature world, with its overflowing bookshelves and window plants and science experiments and small animal cages and rows of desks with chairs atop them (signs of custodial work?) and walls crammed with vigorous artwork.

Breathing hard, Elaine came to the end of the exterior of the long central corridor, and circled back around. This was the home stretch. She had to find someone. She had to get in. She was like her father frantically sprinting from the farmhouse to the ice pond. Failure was not an option.

She heard noise inside. It was the distinctive drone of a vacuum cleaner. What a wonderful sound, she thought. What a lovely noise! Someone was in there vacuuming. She pounded hard on the window.

The custodian came to the rear door.

"What are you doing here so late?" he asked.

"The quilt," she blurted, and raced past him toward her room.

In Room 112, she moved a chair to where the quilt hung, stepped up, and unfastened it from its hooks. She folded it a few times and sprinted out.

The custodian stood in the corridor.

"For Seamus," she said, racing past him again.

"How's he doing?"

She was gone.

• • •

There were several cars in the Farrells' driveway, including an Eagle River police car, when Elaine arrived.

This was the week that Ravenwood sixth graders had been at camp up north near Palmer, where they explored Matanuska Glacier and hiked to the fossil fields. Camp was a traditional three-day overnight outing that the upper grades at Ravenwood went on every spring. Different teachers treated camp differently. Some turned it into a quasi–Outward Bound experience, which is what Elaine, Joan, and Rachel Harrison did with the fourth graders, taking them to Birchwood Camp, where the kids stayed in rustic cabins, went on expeditions to complement their science and outdoor education studies, and reenacted Native American legends around a campfire. Coming as it did in the final weeks of school, camp marked the culmination of a year of dedicated work, and it felt so perfectly Alaskan to do it in the woods, close to the elements that made their lives here special.

When Seamus fell into the coma, Jesse was away at sixth-grade camp. It was his second night there (his first night had been nearly sleepless, since he'd forgotten to bring a pillow) and he was just going to bed in his cabin when Arge walked in. He told Jesse that he needed to get home to Eagle River. Jesse did not have to ask why.

After being contacted by the Farrells with a clear sense that time was of the essence, Arge had arranged to drive Jesse south while Terry Simpson, who was on duty that night at the police station, sped north from Eagle River to meet him halfway. That stretch of rural Alaska road had no convenient signposts or landmarks. Arge arranged to pull over roughly at the halfway point and blink his brights as a signal. It worked.

"What does this mean?" Jesse asked Terry as they sped away with the bubble on her patrol car flashing.

She told him that Seamus was near the end.

• • •

Elaine arrived at the Farrells' the second time. Climbing out of her car, she held the quilt in her arms and moved quickly up the driveway.

Inside, Seamus lay motionless in bed. Jim and Susan were on either side of Seamus, holding him and crying. Jesse and Joseph were nearby.

Dr. Bleivik was also there. On a recent visit, Seamus had asked him about the hereafter.

"Did you like Disney World?" Bleivik found himself saying.

"Sure."

"Well, heaven's even better."

"Really?"

Bleivik, recalling the Kübler-Ross injunction against false promises, felt instantly guilty.

Seamus awaited his reply. Bleivik had no choice. "Yes," he finally said. "Even better."

When Elaine arrived, Bleivik was leaning close to Seamus, talking affectionately, consolingly. Hearing, he knew from past experiences, was the last of the five senses to go. But Seamus was showing no response. His breathing was difficult and came in erratic gulps. His eyes were closed. His skin looked impossibly thin, almost translucent. He appeared lifeless.

Elaine paused a moment at the foot of the bed. The haphazardly folded quilt was in her arms.

She didn't know how long this vigil had been going on, but it seemed as if people were thoroughly drained. There was a heavy and palpable mournfulness in the room. She thought she heard someone whisper, "He's gone."

"Seamus!" Elaine blurted.

Her voice as it emerged was a surprise, even to her. Especially to her! It hardly sounded like her voice. This voice was commanding, emphatic, and loud. It was urgent and forceful.

The voice came again. "Seamus!" she shouted. "Look!"

She raised the quilt above his poor bloated comatose body for him to see—as if he could even see! Again, she pleaded, "Open your eyes, Seamus! Look! Look what the kids made for you!"

And Seamus opened his eyes.

Elaine spread the quilt out before him.

He sat straight up. "They made this for me?" he asked incredulously. "The kids made this for me?"

7

WISH LIST

The word *miracle* was used, but only offhandedly, the way sports fans might casually refer to a dramatic come-from-behind finish by their home team.

Amazing events, of course, could actually happen. Predicted outcomes did undergo sudden shifts. Foregone conclusions did not always play out exactly as expected. Likely developments were nonetheless governed by probability, a law notorious for its loopholes.

It certainly had seemed that Seamus was dying. His breathing had become labored and irregular. His eyes had shut, and stayed shut, for many hours. He had shown no appreciable response to any stimulus, not to touch, not to noise, not to smell. He was, by all accounts, on the brink of death. It had been nearly six months since that awful December day when the tumor was discovered, and not a day had passed for the Farrells when this turn of events, this outcome, this eventuality would have been a surprise. The miracle, Susan and Jim often reminded themselves, was that it had not come sooner.

What exactly happened that May night with Elaine and the quilt?

This much was clear. The teacher entered the room holding a large blanket. People around the bed parted, to give her access to Seamus.

She lifted the blanket, showing its marvelous patterns. Why? It was certainly an odd gesture. Surely she knew Seamus wasn't able to look.

Next, the teacher instructed him—*shouted*—"Look!" This teacher who never raised her voice, who always spoke in velvet tones that were never, ever jarring, this teacher who hardly believed in commanding anyone to do anything, who in fact believed there were more effective means of changing people's behavior, had ordered, yes, *ordered* him to look!

And the boy did just that.

Seamus responded as readily as a child told to spit out his gum. He sat up and immediately started chatting about the quilt. He tried picking out who'd made which squares and showed delight at spotting his own. There was enthusiasm in his voice and a bit of the old sparkle in his eyes. He smiled at those huddled at his bedside and they gratefully welcomed him back.

That is what happened.

Then Susan and Jim showered him with tearful hugs. Jesse and Colin and Joseph pressed closer, greeting him as though he'd returned from a long and perilous voyage. Everyone was joyful, tearful, and phenomenally relieved.

Elaine left the quilt with Seamus and backed away, dazed. She listened as others talked excitedly about answered prayers, and could only agree.

Interpretations of precisely what took place varied.

Disposed to a sort of naturalist spirituality, Joan Johnson felt there was an obvious through-line extending from the heartfelt effort the students had invested in making the quilt straight to Seamus's surprise awakening. "This needed to happen," Joan reasoned. "For the kids and for Seamus. How many of us can honestly say we were ever wrapped with love? Well, that's what the quilt did. What is our fear of dying? Our fear of dying is that we were not loved by other people, that we didn't make a difference, that people didn't care about us. Not with Seamus."

Joan also believed it was skating on thin ice to openly discuss this dimension of what took place. "Elaine might have brought this boy back from death," Joan said. "And you just don't go there."

Dr. Bleivik had been with many people in their final hours. In his experience, this certainly amounted to a dramatic turnaround. But for a spiritual man, he was disinclined to seize on an interpretation that might suggest more than met the eye. Bleivik had had questions about whether

Seamus in his coma was actually dying, and was less surprised than the others when he sat up and spoke.

Bleivik is, however, a firm believer that there are people blessed with healing powers, whether or not they are officially ordained as such and regardless of whether they themselves even know it. He recalled Kübler-Ross's account of a hospital where a number of cancer patients suddenly began showing almost overnight improvement. None of the doctors or hospital staff could figure it out. As it turned out, there was an orderly on the all-night shift who would saunter in during the night and visit with them, talk to them, commune with them, be with them. Nothing formal, nothing specific, nothing prescribed. One of Bleivik's favorite Bible sayings is from Matthew: "We are earthen vessels."

"The teacher," Bleivik said, "was an earthen vessel. The teacher was the priest. On the school side."

Seamus's older brother Joseph, who has a keenly analytic mind, felt there was a convergence of events that were explainable on a physiological basis. For pain medication, Seamus had been given morphine. In Joseph's view, his little brother had experienced something like a narcotic overdose, induced by his weakened state and a faulty prescription. Seamus's revival at that point in time may have been nudged by hearing Elaine's voice but was mostly, according to Joseph, simply a function of a powerful drug wearing off.

Elaine was powerless to explain what had happened. Nor was she inclined to.

Grandiose interpretations of human events, though they surely spice up the plot in storybooks and poems, were not her instinctual way of assessing life's developments. Especially when her own actions were involved. She tended to the view that if one looks closely enough, the world is absolutely teeming with miracles large and small—the salmon spawning, the geology of rivers, a late-afternoon rainbow over the playground. The only reason to make more out of it was our psychological need to do so. Sure, the desire to have life *mean* something beyond what was observable and provable was one that Elaine shared. But wishing it so did not make it a fact.

Elaine preferred to put it this way: something very special had occurred. The kids had made a beautiful quilt. She had managed by the skin of her teeth to deliver it to Seamus's bedside before it was too late. And although it had seemed that he was on the brink of death, now it appeared that he was feeling, well, livelier.

• • •

The very next day, Elaine arranged for the entire class—all twenty-five of them at once—to visit Seamus at lunch hour. This would be the long-awaited Seamus Quilt Day celebration. The school year was winding down. It was now or never.

Soon, word of Seamus's astonishing revival spread throughout Eagle River. Like many a good story, it became the property of the individual teller, but the essence was this: the boy was gone, then he came back, and he wrapped himself in a quilt made for him by his classmates and it couldn't have happened to a nicer kid or a nicer family.

Susan and Jim were flooded with calls of congratulations. It was hard on them to have to point out to well-wishers that "recovery," unfortunately, was probably not the accurate term. Their son was still very, very ill.

But Seamus was markedly improved, and this was evident the day his classmates arrived. He sat in his wheelchair by the upstairs window watching the caravan of cars pull in to the long driveway. The quilt was wrapped around him.

One by one, the children climbed out of the cars, up the few stairs to the front door, then up the stairway to where he sat waiting. No coats or hats or gloves. It was springtime, verging on summer. Leaves were filling out on the trees and the Farrells' lawn was already a vivid green. Boys wore T-shirts. Several girls wore sleeveless blouses that matched their shorts.

Seamus wore the Universal Studios T-shirt he'd picked up in Florida, white with black and purple lettering, and no hat. His hair was reduced mostly to one thick lock swept to cover the forward portion of his scalp. His face glistened and was round as a beach ball. As his classmates swept in, he beamed and gave them a thumbs-up.

They gathered in the living room. Cake and ice cream were served in lieu of lunch. This was a party, and for very good reason. Jim and Susan and Elaine were giddy. One of the parents passed out foil juice pouches. The kids encircled Seamus, who sat on the sofa with the quilt around his shoulders. It had been clasped tight to his body nearly every minute since he'd received it.

"This is for you, Seamus," said Alex, handing him the leather-bound book.

As he was already wrapped in the quilt, today's surprise was the album containing their original crayon squares and the accompanying letters. The book was laid out so that each left-hand page containing a child's letter faced the corresponding drawing on the right-hand page.

Seamus received the album with an outstretched hand. It was heavier than he expected and Lauren Smith, seated beside him, helped adjust it on his lap. Seamus began leafing through it. The kids pressed around him, eager for his reactions, especially when he arrived at their page.

Seamus studied a page showing a big nasty-looking creature. Then he read the note from James Lockwood. "My picture is of a boar because I like boars," said the note.

"Thanks," Seamus said.

Seamus took his time, reading each note, admiring each drawing, glancing up to acknowledge the author/illustrator. "Thanks," he'd say. "It's really nice."

"You like the sharp teeth?"

"You bet."

He went carefully through the album, page by page, classmate by classmate, lingering over each drawing, sight-reading each note. As he came to their respective pages, each child squirmed forward to be closer. There was of course one basic response that the kids wanted from artwork they'd created. And Seamus did not disappoint.

He loved what they did, loved it unequivocally. They could see it in the smile broadening across his face each time he turned the page and came anew to another page, another gift from another friend.

"Wait till you see mine."

"He'll get there."

"I did the alien!"

"Give him time."

Oh yes, time. Seamus was in no hurry. Each drawing, each note was a bridge linking him to the world he loved, the world of Ravenwood School. His family was great. His parents and brothers were as compassionate and fun as a boy could want. But there was a world outside of family, a larger family that had embraced him. It had been his biggest fear when he first learned of the cancer, bigger than his fear of death—the fear that he would no longer be part of Elaine's circle.

That fear had proved false.

Eventually, Seamus came to the last page. Lunch hour had already gone past its allotted time and Seamus, perhaps sensing this, lingered a bit longer, knowing that its conclusion also meant farewell.

Terry Simpson, watching from the stairwell, glanced at Elaine. Probably it was time to wrap this up and proceed back to school. Elaine understood, and nodded. There was work to be done. These twenty-five children who had learned so much this year still had some science and math lessons to master. The school year was winding down, but not yet over. It was time to say good-bye.

"See you soon," they said to Seamus.

"We'll be back," they said.

"Come visit," they said.

"We love you, Seamus," they said.

They cleaned up the refuse from their snacks, stuffing the deflated juice pouches and crumpled bags of chips in a garbage bag. They bantered among themselves, about Little League baseball, about a *Jurassic Park* sequel everyone wanted to see, about who would sit with whom on the ride back. They started down the stairs.

Seamus was alone on the sofa now, holding the book. The quilt on his lap was turned around. Only its black sashing showed.

"I can't see the pictures," Elaine said, as she started down the stairs.

"I want the pictures next to me," Seamus answered.

• • •

And then it was summer.

Just like that, or so it seemed, the school year was over and the splendid season of sunlight and vacation was upon them. Every academic year begins with hope and in a perfect world concludes with it also. It had been, from Elaine's viewpoint, a remarkable class. Whether that was due to unique characteristics of the individual children, unique features of their group dynamics or, as she was prone to believe, the fact that ordinary children always have within them the capacity to rise to extraordinary situations, was a question Elaine would have time to consider over the coming months. Until summer's end, when a new class with the bright eager faces of new kids began the seasonal swim into her life.

These kids this year, these kids who'd had fun and kept pace with their schoolwork and mastered long division and the scientific names for bones, who'd acquired a keen appreciation for the traditions and culture of native Alaskans and still were able to dedicate themselves to a dying classmate, would all move on to the fifth grade. They would see each other at recess, pass each other in the hallways, play with each other on after-school sports teams, and in groups of five or six they would even remain together in some other teacher's classroom in the coming years. But as a group, as a whole, as twenty-five children in the same room, with the same teacher, in the same circle, the last day of school in early June was their final day.

(Well, almost. Remember the grant the kids had been awarded to rebuild the vandalized amphitheater? Until now, there'd been no chance to actually do the repair work. The grounds had been covered with snow until recently, and then it had become difficult to mobilize everyone at the same time, what with the accumulating busyness of spring.

The only way to get the work done was *after* the end of the school year. And that's what they all did. The afternoon of the day that school let out for summer vacation, the kids stayed late at Ravenwood, working in the warm sun under Elaine's supervision, with the assistance of parents, grandparents, and siblings. The restored amphitheater would be ready for fall.)

The saddest day of the year, Elaine often thought, was that day in early June when school was done until fall and she would be alone in Room 112, clearing out. Every year it was so, a bittersweet culmination. Her sadness at their moving on was of course mixed with happiness for them as they went. The emptiness she felt at their absence would in time be filled by an incoming class. That was a teacher's cycle, up and down and around and back. Ending in June to start anew in the fall.

As Elaine packed up the room, she was reminded again of the ways that teaching kids is so very different from parenting them, although comparisons between the two are often made. She would of course see these kids again. Ravenwood was small, and she would run into all of them many times as they progressed through fifth and sixth grade. Eagle River was small, and she would run into all of them, and their parents, at some point or another. One of the unique features of Eagle River was that most of the teachers lived in town.

In fact, Ravenwood teachers sometimes complained that they couldn't go to Carrs grocery store—or even Tips, the tavern—without running into an impromptu parent-teacher conference. "Going to the store with my mother felt like being with a movie star," recalled Elaine's daughter Michelle. "People were always coming up to us and saying how great she was. Stuff like, 'Our Jimmy couldn't even read, and now he's in graduate school!'"

Even when they left Ravenwood she would be kept apprised, if only in sketchy detail, of her former students' middle school careers, as well as their time at Chugiak High School. She liked to go to their high school graduations, to show support, to add continuity. She wanted her former students to go on to perform well, to retain the love of learning she'd worked so hard to instill. She wanted her students to explore the world and explore themselves and be good people to those around them and in the larger communities of which she hoped they now understood themselves to be a part.

Beyond that, Elaine had no burning maestro's desire to launch a prodigy or cultivate a superstar who, years hence, in accepting the Nobel or Pulitzer or Oscar, would remember to thank her for all she had done. Her objective was more modest, and more real. "We teach," explained Joan Johnson, speaking of Elaine and herself and others, "to create these kids who can go on and do life better."

• • •

The Farrells made the most of the unfolding weeks of summer, as long as it lasted.

Seamus had always enjoyed bike riding, and the previous summer had marked the first year that his parents allowed the boys to ride beyond shouting distance from the house. Suddenly Jesse and Seamus had had access to the whole of the valley, so long as they were careful and looked both ways. What liberation! They could visit friends without a ride from Mom or Dad. They could cruise the quiet side streets off Eagle River Road, pretending to be commandos on patrol. They could glide effortlessly down the mammoth hills. (Though invariably they had to climb back up.)

This summer, due to the deterioration of his leg muscles, Seamus could not do it. Once again, he was confined to the yard. On his good days, he was able to maneuver on his scooter for a bit in the driveway. But mostly he had to settle for watching his brothers zip around.

Debbie Peters, Laura's mother, was driving one warm summer evening and saw a figure on a bicycle. The mountain peaks of Sleeping Lady were visible in the distance. The figure on the bike was grinding up the hill with a grueling pumping motion, making hardly any progress, like the mythical Sisyphus rolling a boulder uphill. Coming closer, Debbie saw it was Jim Farrell, his cheeks flushed with exertion, pedaling Seamus, all 150 pounds of him, who was strapped into a child's covered carryall that Jim had fastened to the rear of his bike. Passing them as they continued their impossible uphill struggle, Debbie became choked with emotion. "They were making such an incredible effort," she recalled thinking, "to have Seamus experience a normal life."

In June, after school had let out and there were no more regular visits from the kids, Seamus made out a list of things he wanted to do. He wrote this down on a sheet of notebook paper with faint blue horizontal lines in the careful cursive he'd learned, but not yet perfected, at Ravenwood. He gave the paper to his mother and watched her expression as she read it.

"Can I?" he asked her.

"We'll see," Susan said. "We'll have to see." And she read the list again.

He wanted to watch cartoons with his brothers.

He wanted to go to Bosco's and get some new comic books.

He wanted to see Fourth of July fireworks.

He wanted to go back east to visit his relatives in New Jersey.

He wanted to go camping in the wilderness.

He wanted to catch fish.

He wanted to go to fifth grade.

●　●　●

Susan's brother Bill lived in Freehold, New Jersey, and had children in age ranges compatible with the Farrell boys. The Farrells had been there several years previously and Seamus had fond memories of carefree frolic with cousins who also liked to make mischief and have fun.

Jim was granted several weeks' leave from the Alaska state

troopers and late in June the family flew east. Seamus was spirited, but at times very weak. Susan's brother had made arrangements with a New Jersey home hospice agency, just in case.

The highlight of their stay was the Independence Day fireworks. Due to the nearly perpetual sunlight of mid-summer, Alaskans don't generally experience the Fourth of July fireworks displays that are such a staple of the holiday experience in the Lower 48. It just does not get dark early enough in the summer. (There are, of course, patriotic Alaskans who are determined to have the fireworks anyway, no matter how difficult they are to see against an undark-ened sky.)

Colin stayed home with Aunt Dolores. They weren't going to make that mistake again. The rest of the family and their cousins drove to a nearby park that had an annual Independence Day extravaganza. Susan's brother knew a local police officer who was able to secure for Seamus, and the Farrells, a front-row view.

The flares bursting in air. The night exploding in light. Eyes wide with wonder. The dull percussive thuds from the barge off shore. The salt taste on the warm breeze. The oohs and aahs and giddy shrieks from the delighted chil-dren. Seamus was thrilled to be among them.

In August, back in Alaska, the family went camping up at Boyd's Lake by Palmer. Bob Boyd was a Department of Corrections official Jim knew who owned a great piece of property by a man-made lake stocked with trout that afforded the pleasures of camping—thick woods, proximity to high mountains, fishing—without being impossibly removed. Jim was not an especially avid outdoorsman, certainly not by rugged Alaskan standards. He was not a hunter, not a wilderness backpacker, not a self-reliant survivalist. And not a savvy fisherman. Despite these shortcomings, he liked to joke that he'd figured out how to fake it, at least conversationally.

"All you have to do," he explained, "is ask three questions, and people just figure you're one of them. How much of a fight did he put up? What kind of lure are you using? What pound test?"

But fishing was something his boys loved and he would do anything—even fishing—for them. Even fishing in the rain. The boys had a blast at Boyd's. They carved spears from tree branches and tried their hand—without even a hint of success—at spearfishing. Jesse had a BB gun and, employing solid twelve-year-old logic, tried shooting the fish that swam near the surface. One shot skimmed off the water and plunked Colin, standing nearby, on the arm. The shot raised only a harmless welt but ended, at least temporarily, any fishing except by means of bait and hook.

As the summer progressed, Susan and Jim began to notice subtle changes in Seamus, and not just in the precarious matter of his physical health. He started listening to classical music on the radio, at times preferring the flowing moods of symphony orchestras to the noisy pulse of rock and roll that had previously been his only musical interest.

He'd always been an empathetic boy, a quality honed through his brother-protector relationship to Colin. Now he began to show this side of himself in ways that could only be called artistic.

On the living-room coffee table, he constructed a diorama. The landscape consisted of a hill and a field and a house. Into this world he put plastic figures of both aliens and human beings, purchased at Bosco's. Like a dramatist, he invented imaginative dilemmas that required the warring aliens and humans to cooperate. Susan recalled how he fashioned a roundish clod of clay—an asteroid?—and plunked it into the landscape so the aliens and humans had to join forces to push it up the hill—because it was poisonous? radioactive?—and thereby remove the dire threat from their shared yet fragile world.

He was not forgotten by his classmates.

"He never lost his childhood," Jim reflected. "He'd been petrified that he would lose his friends. And he didn't."

But over the summer, many were busy with the usual summer activities. Some were off for weeks to the Lower 48 visiting their own extended families. Some were busy with scouting and family camping of their own. Others played soccer and baseball and were consumed with practices and games.

Laura Peters and her mom stopped by a couple of times— they lived nearby—with meals or snacks. One afternoon late in August, they went on a whim to Carrs grocery store and picked up pizza for the Farrells, along with a promotional balloon Carrs was giving out. Susan escorted them in to see Seamus, but he was sound asleep in his hospital bed in the living room, and would not awaken. It was a shock for Laura to see him like that, looking so lifeless. They tied the balloon to the headboard and left.

On August 26, Seamus turned eleven and a party was held at the Chugiak High School swimming pool.

The idea was to invite all his friends from Room 112, but some were out of town in this final week before the start of school. Still, nearly twenty kids were able to come.

It was, of course, also the birthday party for Colin, his identical twin. As kids splashed and hollered and swam, Seamus and Colin perched on the pool's edge, their legs dangling in the mild chlorine water. Each wore a yellow life preserver—they were the only children at the party to do so. Colin's motor skills were such that he was not a reliable swimmer, and water could scare him. Seamus, with his deteriorated muscles and bloated body, was not capable of keeping himself afloat. He kept his black FBI cap on his head and was happy to watch from the water's edge, calling out wisecracks to his pals and posing, with his arm around them or theirs around him, for the many snapshots that were taken. Next week, school would start again.

After the party, Seamus told his mother how happy he was. He'd managed to do most of the activities from his start-of-the-summer wish list. There was but one item yet to be done.

• • •

Susan had hoped to bring Seamus to Ravenwood during the first week of school, just after Labor Day. As far as he was concerned, he had successfully completed the fourth grade and was enrolled in the fifth, assigned to the class of Dan Carey. A handsome, voluble, witty, extroverted teacher, Mr. Carey had a schoolwide reputation for being "fun." He had the instincts, mostly latent, of a nightclub comedian, and was known to walk on stilts and dress up as the Jolly Green Giant to entertain at school functions. Dan was in charge of the fifth-grade program in sex education, or "Human Growth and Development" as it was called, and had the kind of rapport with kids that enabled him to turn this most problematic and awkward of topics into the necessary subject matter it had to be. The word was out among fifth graders: Mr. Carey will answer *any* question!

There was never a sense on Susan or Jim Farrell's part, or on that of Arge Jeffery and the Ravenwood administration, that Seamus was a legitimately enrolled fifth grader. This year was not to begin where the last one had left off. There would be no regular mobilization of student visits to his house, no sustained effort to keep him up to speed with his classwork. Each year was different. Each class was different. Resources were in short supply, and so was time.

It was understood, however, that Seamus could come to

school whenever he felt up to it. If he could make it to school, a place would be found for him.

During the second week of school, Seamus was barely able to get out of bed. He was periodically wracked by vomiting and his kidneys were rapidly failing.

Pat Burry, the home health nurse, was around nearly all the time these days. Tending to the terminally ill was her job. In her experience, people who were dying generally knew it. Sometimes this came out conversationally. Sometimes it was just a subconscious awareness, an intuition that required no verbal expression. Her job, she felt, was to validate that apprehension. Seamus, she was starting to realize, had arrived at that point.

But he retained his sense of humor. One evening in September, the Farrell family was gathered somberly in the living room as Seamus slept. The family, Pat noted, was hardly ever morose. Friends visited often. They ordered in pizza. "Sometimes people close the curtains," Pat observed. "The Farrells never did."

Colin began pacing around Seamus's bed. As Seamus faltered, Colin became frightened and confused. "Is he dead yet?" Colin suddenly blurted.

Even Pat gasped.

Seamus struggled to prop himself up. After a perfectly timed pause, he looked his twin directly in the eye. "No, I am not dead yet!"

Seamus smiled, letting them know it was OK to laugh. Everyone but Colin did.

• • •

On the Friday of the third week of school, Seamus told his mother he would like to go to school. He had hardly been out of bed all week, and Susan questioned whether he was truly up to it.

"Are you sure?" she asked warily.

"Yes, I want to go to school today."

Susan had no choice. She helped Seamus wash up and dress. She called the school to double-check that it would be OK. She rolled his wheelchair outside and hoisted it into their sturdy station wagon. She helped Seamus into the passenger seat, and made sure to buckle him in for safety.

"Are you sure you're up to this?" she asked once more.

"Yes," he answered.

Susan hoped the visit would be low-key. She questioned how much Seamus was able to withstand. On the ride over, she explained that they wouldn't stay long. They would go see some of his friends. He did not have to do anything he did not feel up to doing.

Susan pulled up along the curb where the buses parked. Louis, the custodian whose erratic work habits were a source of some in-house amusement, was eagerly waiting in his neatly pressed jeans and sport shirt. He helped Susan unload the wheelchair and took charge of easing Seamus in.

"I'll do it," Louis told Susan.

To Seamus, Louis said, "Hey dude, let's go!" and whisked him into the school.

Susan had to hustle to keep up.

Principal Jeffery and the school nurse, Debbie Corral, were at the front door to greet Seamus.

"Great to see you," Arge told him.

"Great to be here," Seamus replied.

Louis was itching to get moving, but Susan caught up. She knew her son's limitations. "Seamus," she said, "do you want to go see Mrs. Moore first? I know she'd love to see you."

"No, Mom. I'm in fifth grade. I want to go to Mr. Carey's class."

"You won't know all the kids there."

"It's all right. I'll meet new friends."

Susan glanced at Arge. Arge nodded to Louis. And away they went.

Younger kids, second graders judging by their size, were spilling out of the gymnasium as Seamus rolled by. They reached out as he passed to slap his outstretched hand like teammates from the sideline.

Louis wheeled him past the stained-glass map of Alaska, past the cross-country ski rack, past the art room with its display case featuring recently glazed and kilned ceramics, past the resource room where his brother Colin might be at this very moment, past the library with its comfortable cushioned reading nooks and fabric mural of the winding Eagle River valley.

In Room 112, Elaine was busily initiating a new crop of fourth graders. They'd already had several hikes in the woods around Ravenwood. She'd introduced them to

Circle Time. They were learning the fundamentals of how to create their own celebrations. They had been told that learning was an activity meant to last a lifetime.

Elaine had been notified that Seamus was coming to Ravenwood. Like the proverbial configurations of snowflakes, no two school years were the same. This year would not be like last year, and last year had been like no other. Seamus had moved beyond Room 112, a long way beyond. It was OK by her if he preferred to spend his visit in Mr. Carey's class. We all move along, Elaine couldn't help but reflect. Even when we're going in circles.

• • •

In Mr. Carey's room, Seamus was given his own desk to sit at. Dan introduced him to the class, but did not make a big deal out of it. Dan had decided to treat this like normal class time. In fact, based on a conversation he'd had with the school nurse, Dan believed that was Seamus's fondest wish, to be a normal student in a normal class for as long as he could manage it.

Several of his Room 112 classmates were enrolled in Mr. Carey's class. Other kids knew who he was. As Seamus went to take his seat at his assigned desk, moving unsteadily down the aisle in his wheelchair, children pushed chairs aside to ease his passage. But there was no special fuss beyond that. Some kids said, "Hi, how're you doing?" Seamus only smiled in reply. He was back at school, and he wanted to show respect.

Susan waited outside the room, warily observing the class. She studied his face for signs of when she would need to retrieve him. Did he look shaky or nauseous or troubled? But Seamus was listening too intently to whatever Mr. Carey was saying to return her glance.

The class was doing spelling practice. Mr. Carey handed out work sheets to the kids in the front row of desks, and the sheets were passed backward. Seamus, in a middle row, took a sheet for himself and passed on the rest to the next desk back. He knew the drill. This was what he wanted.

Next, Mr. Carey directed the class to their social studies books. The early American colonial experience was their focus during these first weeks of the school year. There was a passage about the importance of freedom to the early settlers that he wanted the class to discuss. But first they had to read it, to themselves, at their desks. Mr. Carey gave them ten minutes to do so. Seamus did not hesitate. He opened his book, just like everyone else, and began to read.

Elaine came by to join Susan in the hall outside Mr. Carey's room.

"How's he doing?" she asked.

"Right now?" Susan answered. "Right now, just fine."

Mother and teacher pressed closer to the door to watch. Seamus was in his wheelchair at a desk—*his desk*—on which there was an open textbook. He looked up at this new teacher. He looked down at the book. His eyes darted about, assessing his new classmates. For this frozen instant in time, he appeared to be a normal kid in a friendly environment.

And he was very happy.

When it was time to leave, Louis was right there again, as if on cue. He took charge of wheeling Seamus back out to the parking lot. Students and teachers in the hallways again reached out, slapping him five as he passed. Susan bustled alongside.

Melissa O'Guin was standing right outside the school office as Seamus rolled by. "See you in heaven," he said to her cheerily.

Once outside, Seamus turned to his mom with a satisfied smile.

"I did it, Mom," he beamed. "I did everything on my list! Can you believe it? I made it to fifth grade!"

• • •

Two days later, he died peacefully at home.

8

MEMORIAL

T his account about a teacher, a student, a school, and the surrounding community could end at this point. The class of fourth graders had moved on to fifth. The teacher who'd done all she could, as she always did, was immersed in the challenges of a fresh group of students who'd gone already to Eagle River Nature Center, where they'd become acquainted with the life cycle of the remarkable salmon and learned to "spot it!"

The boy in the story, sadly, had passed away.

But there remained the matter of a memorial service. The standard venue for such an event would be a church or a funeral parlor, and in their grief the Farrells briefly considered these options. But Susan and Jim had decided on cremation rather than burial, and had lapsed far enough from mainstream religious faith, despite the ministrations of Dr. Bleivik, that a formal ceremony involving heavy rituals whose symbolism they did not fully subscribe to did not seem the best way to say good-bye to their son.

The best way, Susan and Jim agreed, would be amid a swarm of friends in a familiar setting: Ravenwood School.

During condolence calls, Susan had mentioned to several parents that, unorthodox as it sounded, the school was the only venue that fit the family's criteria. They wanted a space large enough to accommodate many people, for this was not to be a private affair, and they wanted a place that Seamus had loved as a second home.

However, there were regulations to consider.

Private use of public buildings can be a complicated procedure, with liability concerns always lurking in the background. Additionally, public schools are not eager to get into the thorny business of being used for religious purposes. And there is always the worry of establishing a precedent that might precipitate further requests, further complications.

The matter of Seamus's memorial needed to be settled quickly. Elaine went to Arge with the request. He said it was simply not possible.

She enlisted the help of several teachers and parents, who lobbied the principal.

Arge was worried about setting a thorny precedent. "What's going to happen," he pointed out, "if other families want to use the school in this way?"

"Give me a break," Joan complained. "How many kids die in elementary school?"

"Well, what about outside groups? We're a public facility, you know."

"We don't have time for this discussion," Joan argued. "We only have enough time to do this right."

Arge came around. It had been a year of learning—even for the school principal. "I tried to maintain normalcy, yet stay sensitive to what was taking place," he said of the dilemma he faced.

For the kids, there was a comforting aspect to holding the service at Ravenwood. "I was horrified at the idea of going to a funeral," said Alex Vanderhoff, "but there, where we'd had all those assemblies, it was OK."

● ● ●

The service was set to begin at 7 PM on Friday evening with a potluck meal to follow (the printed announcement stated, "According to your last name, please bring: A–I Salad; J–R Main Dish; S–Z Dessert").

From the long line of cars and SUVs streaming down Wren Lane into the Ravenwood parking lot, one might guess that a pop music event was scheduled, or some massive town-wide meeting on a hot-button issue. Once the parking lot had filled up, vehicles backed onto the unpaved perimeter by the hockey rink. When that area too was filled, they circled back to the entrance road and pulled onto the shoulder.

The Farrell family arrived in a Dodge minivan that had been rented by Uncle Bill, who had flown in from New Jersey. They were escorted to the principal's office to wait in privacy until the service began. Jesse could hear throngs of people streaming into the school. It felt like being back-stage before the start of an important event.

Inside the gymnasium, parents who'd shuttled kids to the lunchtime visits and found themselves in weighty dinner-table talks that had initially made them squirm, but for which they now were grateful, gladly pitched in. They grabbed metal folding chairs off the carts wedged in the corner and, along with Louis, who'd stayed long after his normal quitting time, they arranged these in tight rows. They shepherded children to the front, where they would sit on the floor until the service began.

All the kids were there: Paul Hackenmueller who a decade later would be a math major at Colorado State University; Hans Bernard, who would spend a semester studying democratic practices in South Africa while an undergraduate at Willamette University; Danielle White-head, who would teach English for a year in the Ukraine before returning to study physical therapy at Brigham Young University; Jake Simpson, who would retreat to his bedroom in the coming days to write a poem to ease his sorrow ("When the sky is blue and clouds are white and days are getting colder . . .") and go on to be certified as an air-traffic controller; Alex Vanderhoff, who would struggle through adolescence before becoming a competitive bike racer and mechanical engineering student at the University of Nevada–Reno; Cullen Kurzmann, who would leave college in Michigan to try his hand at a start-up business, hoping to replicate in the Midwest the popularity of Alaska-style drive-up coffee shacks; Laura Peters, who, as a college accounting major working part-time in her father's automotive-parts business would occasionally find herself telling people who were not from Eagle River, new friends from her expanding world, about that amazing year when she was a young girl in the fourth grade. No, no, don't get me wrong, she would assure the listener. Sad things happened and, yes, the story could be construed as depressing. But amazingly, it never was. Even as she might tear up telling it, she would insist the story was really quite uplifting.

All the students from Room 112 would have versions of this experience, of being prompted years later—by a fleeting memory or a chance observation, say, of a child in a wheelchair—into reflecting on that remarkable year when they were ten and one of their classmates was stricken with cancer. They would recall how their teacher made the ongoing inclusion of their ailing friend the centerpiece of their class and how, after he passed away, the school hosted a funeral service that was—hard to believe—a celebration.

New acquaintances to whom they might tell this story would question it. "Come on, a celebration?"

"Yes, that's what it was. Any day, you know, can be cause for a celebration."

Saying Good-bye to Seamus Day.

People flooded into the Ravenwood gym. They poured through every entrance. Teachers and staff who'd been close to the previous year's events became ushers, directing people to vacant seats. Joan, of course, and Rachel Harrison and Peggy Kurzmann and Dan Carey and Melissa O'Guin helped prepare the stage. Bouquets of flowers were distributed across the lip of the stage, yellow daisies and white roses and blooms that were violet and blue. Flanking the flowers, in a neat row, were the caps, two dozen of them, that Seamus had worn to cover his disfigured scalp over his months of illness—LAPD, FBI, USAF, California Highway Patrol, FBI Alaska. Also in a row onstage were all his stuffed animals, those frayed and worn comfort objects that had kept him company since infancy. The big white bear, mysteriously delivered to him after his surgery, was there as well for all to see.

At the conclusion of the service, as people damped their tears and hugged each other and damped their tears again, Seamus's former classmates would be encouraged to come to the stage. They would be told that the Farrell family, expressing Seamus's wish, hoped they would each take one of his stuffed animals or one of his special caps or flowers from the bouquets onstage. And the children would do so.

Directly in front of the stage was a simple card table, covered by a cloth of patchwork stars. On it was a framed photograph of Seamus.

In the picture, the portrait photographer's artificial backdrop was a vivid sky blue. Seamus wore a bright blue sweatshirt that highlighted the pink of his skin and his unkempt sweep of brown hair. This was his official fourth-grade class picture, taken, along with that of all the other Room 112 kids, on a designated day the previous fall when all the children's faces were scrubbed and Seamus was healthy and boyishly thin.

It was the sort of designated class-picture day that is virtually a ritual in schools throughout America. Earnest parents notified by teachers try their best to get their child to wear something presentable and clean. Teachers nudged by photographers remind their students to look straight into the camera and smile. Click!

Some manage it better than others. In the photos that year of Elaine Moore's fourth-grade class, taken on an autumn afternoon in the multipurpose room when the class was still in its formative stages, when the kids were just getting to know the unusual ways of their teacher and were starting to have an inkling, but only an inkling, of the adventures that awaited them, the children appear scrubbed and happy. These were good kids who pretty much knew what the photographer wanted, namely eye contact and a pleasant expression. Scan their pictures, all twenty-five of them (Erik Johnson, who did not join the class until after Christmas break, missed out on photo day), and those are the qualities that would leap out: pleasantness, sincerity, a hint of whimsy, a hint of something that might be called seriousness.

Only one student of the Room 112 group looked in his photos to be really, truly, fully having fun. That was Seamus, and if you looked at that picture or, when he was alive, looked into his face, you would be powerless to do anything but laugh right along with him. The photograph of that laughing face, pink against a backdrop of blue, beamed upon the people filling up Ravenwood's gym.

Behind Seamus's photo, attached to the pleated beige stage curtain, hung the quilt.

Later, after the memorial service concluded, Kay Pederson, whose son AJ would go to college at Minot State University in North Dakota and enlist in the U.S. Army Reserves with an eye toward a career in military intelligence, would spot a school custodian taking down the quilt. The man was not, Kay was alarmed to see, doing it properly. He was treating the quilt as if it were an ordinary blanket set to go into storage. Kay would impulsively rush to the stage, snatch the quilt away, and proceed to fold it the right way, in careful thirds, with dignity and reverence, the way the flag is treated by the military.

• • •

The memorial service called for readings from Psalm 23 and Psalm 90 ("So teach us to number our days, that we may apply our hearts unto wisdom"). Dr. Bleivik was to deliver a sermon titled "My two buddies," referring to Seamus and Jesus. A large chorus of Room 112 classmates and other Ravenwood students was to sing "Love in Any Language," including sign language. This, more than any other feature of the deeply moving service, would send tears splashing down cheeks, including those of career-military dads.

There would be an interlude for people to offer personal remarks or reminiscences. There would be, according to the printed program notes, "A word from his teacher."

The room was filled beyond capacity, beyond fire code capacity, with over 750 people. Teachers stood by the entrance, directing late arrivals to the few remaining chairs. An announcement was made for people to please do their best to squeeze together and make as much room as possible for the kids seated on the floor in front and the grown-ups forced to stand in the rear. One of the parents asked where Elaine was.

"She's over . . ." Joan surveyed the overflow crowd and realized with some consternation that she didn't see Elaine anywhere.

"Hmmm. That's odd." Joan went into the hallway to look for Elaine.

Joan combed the corridor. She checked the school office, and the PTA office across the hall. She peeked into the faculty lounge and glanced in the library. Finally she found Elaine, looking lost and alone, in Room 112.

She was at her desk. The room was empty.

"Let's get going," Joan urged.

"I can't."

"What do you mean you can't?" There was impatience in Joan's voice.

"I don't know what to say."

"I thought you told me you wrote some notes."

"I left my reading glasses at home."

Joan could hardly believe she was hearing this—Elaine Moore resorting to a dog-ate-my-homework type of excuse? "You have to," Joan insisted.

This year with Seamus had been too vital and too wrenching for her to summarize. Elaine felt helpless. "I . . . I just can't."

"For Seamus, Elaine. You have to do it for Seamus."

Elaine, of course, knew that this was so.

She and Joan walked down the corridor to the overflowing gymnasium. Elaine carried several sheets of paper that she would use when it was time for her to speak. She had, in fact, left her reading glasses at home. The papers on which her notes were written would function as Dumbo's feather, giving nothing more than reassurance when reassurance was all that was needed. She clutched the papers.

The service began.

Jim Farrell had written a tribute to his son, but he was too choked with emotion to read it. He handed it to his brother Dan, who'd flown in from Seattle. "Still," Dan read from Jim's notes, "Seamus accepted this whole new sad life as he did any challenge—with a smile and a twinkle in his eye."

Dr. Bleivik had worn an especially colorful tie and as he stepped forward to speak, Jesse, doing his best to be the good boy he knew he should be, marveled at its flashiness. He was tempted to chuckle. There was something almost goofy about the tie. It was the exact opposite of funeral.

Bleivik's talk, "My two buddies," was a continuation of one of his pet themes, the everyday presence of religion in people's lives. He recounted his conversations with Seamus over the past nine months and spoke of how they'd come to be—there really was no better word for it—buddies. He spoke of Seamus's strength and courage and spirit. And then he related what he had told Seamus: that he, Bleivik, had another buddy who possessed those very same qualities, and his name was Jesus. A buddy that he shared with Jesus—it had pleased Seamus to think of Dr. Bleivik that way.

"And now," Bleivik said, "A word from Seamus's teacher."

Elaine stepped up to the podium, situated in front of the stage. She had been in this same position many times before, at holiday pageants and choral programs and other school assemblies, but never with so many in attendance. There were parents of children and friends of the Farrells. There were Alaska state troopers and fellow nursing students of Susan's. Doctors from Providence Medical Center were there, along with the entire Ravenwood faculty and school staff. There were children from all grades, dozens of kids who knew Seamus or Colin or Jesse. Now they waited for Elaine.

Standing at the podium, Elaine knew it would be best to speak in a forceful voice that could project to the back. But she could only do what—with one glaring exception—she had always done. She could only speak in the calm voice that asserted itself in that special way that the purest quiet sometimes has of outperforming thunder.

Yes, she acknowledged, she had been Seamus Farrell's teacher. It had been a privilege to know him, and in saying that she believed she also spoke for the twenty-five children who had been in her class with him last year. All the kids from that class were here this evening, and Elaine paused a moment to scan the rows where the chorus sat. Her panic at speaking before such a large audience was starting to ease. She said:

"It is so fitting that we are gathered here tonight in Seamus's school. Seamus didn't just come to school; he burst into the room every morning with his irresistible grin and the 'I love life' twinkle in his eye. We began every day in our class with Circle Time. This was a time when we'd sit in a circle and share with each other. When he burst into the room, he never failed to say, 'Mrs. Moore, I've got something for Circle Time!' And believe me, he always did. It was Seamus's favorite time of the day.

"Jim and Susan tell of his tree-climbing adventures. He'd climb to the highest branches until they grew too spindly to hold him—resulting in a call to 911. He loved anything that flew—airplanes, space monsters, aliens.

"Seamus had a wonderful sense of humor. I remember the first week in my class. He wrote in his learning log about not liking the activities, our class, even going so far as to say he didn't like school. I was shocked! Here was a kid who was electric with enthusiasm. Then I turned the page and he had written 'NOT' with twenty-three exclamation marks!

"But most important to Seamus were his friends, and he was a friend to everyone he met. He taught us what it meant to be a friend. If someone couldn't find their pencil, Seamus was the first to offer one of his. If someone forgot their lunch, he would share his."

Elaine was calm now. She'd found her voice. Everyone, children and grown-ups, was perfectly still, perfectly silent, perfectly in tune with her words.

"The kids in our class last year gave a lot to Seamus," Elaine said. "But he gave them—and all of us—so much more. From him they learned about death and dying. But most of all, *he* taught *us* about courage and how to live."

Looking across the crowd, from the Ravenwood kids sitting cross-legged in the front rows to the teachers and parents and neighbors filling every chair, standing in the rear and packing the aisles, Elaine half wished she could do what she did better than anything else: gather them all into a circle and coax a conversation that would meander around to what was always, regardless of topic and regardless of content, the prevailing theme: our lives are connected, and that is a very, very good thing.

We are all, she liked to think, salmon swimming boldly out to sea, hoping to return some distant day to a safe place.

Her heart was full. But words did come. In fact, it seemed as though she had the capacity to speak for hours.

But that would be what another speaker, another teacher, might do.

Elaine Moore simply said, "Thank you, Seamus."

And returned to her seat.

AUTHOR'S NOTE

T his book wouldn't have been possible had not several people who had good reason to remain private about an extremely painful episode not chosen instead to discuss their experiences in great detail and with a depth of feeling. Nobody ever explicitly said, "Seamus would have wanted us to tell you this," but I had a clear sense that many I interviewed were moved by something approximating that thought. And rightly so, I hope.

I am most grateful to the Farrell family, and especially to Colin Farrell who was brave until the day he died, in the fall of 2004, from complications related to a brain tumor similar to the one that afflicted Seamus. Colin developed into a proud and impressive young man who was a source of inspiration to everyone who knew him.

In the weeks leading up to his death, at the age of twenty-two, a psychologist was enlisted to help Colin withstand the terror of knowing his untimely end was near. (He was diagnosed with the brain tumor at the age of eighteen; it was thought to have been eradicated, and then reemerged.) As a means of coming to terms with his fears, the psychologist helped Colin write a memoir of his life, illustrated with photographs. One photo depicts him beside Seamus, playing in the snow with Eagle River's magnificent glacial peaks as the backdrop. No two boys ever looked happier.

Colin's short memoir, which he titled "My Life," is heartbreaking to read, and one can only imagine how terribly difficult it was to write. It begins, "My identical twin, Seamus, died from cancer and I fought horrible feelings after that and I survived. Now I am fighting brain cancer." On a later page, Colin writes, "I am not ready to die yet, so I resist this slipping away. I want to die peaceably, to have a good crossing. But I'm not sure how to do that."

Susan and Jim Farrell were far more helpful than I had any right to expect. It cannot be pleasant to recall in painstaking detail the circumstances surrounding the death of a child. To do so, as the Farrells did with me, at a time when another child is imperiled is . . . well, words cannot express it. Their magnificent spirit and remarkable fortitude were vital to this project.

Elaine Moore's contributions are too numerous to itemize. In addition to her patience with my multitude of questions, some of which were asked more than once, she agreed to review portions of the manuscript. And I have a mass of notations—handwritten in a perfect red-ink cursive—scrunched in the margins of a preliminary draft to prove it!

It was an interesting psychodynamic, having a manuscript read by a skilled teacher torn between the extreme discomfort of seeing herself portrayed in a way that is, to put it mildly, at odds with her instinctual self-effacement ("Why can't you use a made-up name for the teacher?" she kept nudging me) and, on the other hand, being subjected to her equally strong urge to correct spelling errors, punctuation, choice of words, and plain old facts. At one point, as I anxiously awaited Elaine's comments, I realized that I was back in my old grade-school mindset, longing primarily for one response: I wanted the teacher to declare that my work was wonderful and draw a great big smiley face atop the first page. I never did get that—talk about a tough grader!—but what I did receive from Elaine was far more important.

In the course of researching this book, I traveled twice to Eagle River and met many current and former Ravenwood teachers, not all of whom are mentioned by name. Those I did meet struck me as exceptionally bright, engaged, and high-spirited, with varied interests and a love of the outdoors. They are also a lot of fun. One evening, we gathered for what I thought would be a group interview session. To be fair, the teachers might have initially seen it that way, also. But once they assembled around a sumptuous potluck feast and a—is it OK to use the term "healthy"?—supply of beer and wine, the interview session deteriorated (or accelerated) into a great party. My notes from that evening record numerous deft one-liners (Dan Carey, having just returned from a weekend in Homer, Alaska, referred to it as "a quaint drinking town with a fishing problem") and the sort of swapped group-participation stories that only trusting friends can generate. How a small-town elementary school in an isolated region managed to recruit and develop such an extraordinary staff is an interesting topic that I considered trying to address. But that would be another book. For now, I thank them all.

Vicky Bennet assisted with valuable background research in several key areas and provided me with the kind of close, thoughtful, sensitive reading of the manuscript in draft phase that every writer craves.

George Greenfield helped convince me that this outline of a story, really no more than a sketch, could become a book, and then he put his shoulder into the effort and found a publisher for it.

Matthew Lore is that publisher. I am immensely thankful to him for having the vision and heart to understand that this nonfiction work that falls into no fashionable publishing category—with no dastardly crime or cataclysmic disaster or overexposed celebrity as its centerpiece—was worthy of his support. Seeking a commercial hook, as anyone involved in the business of publishing must be, Matthew kept trying to conjure up a category, some equivalent to the successful True Crime genre, that would embrace this book. True Good People? True Lives to Learn From? Real Life Saints? We're still open to suggestions.

My interest in this project was whetted before I knew about Elaine Moore. At Bowman Elementary School in Lexington, Massachusetts, my sons, Louis and Daniel, were fortunate enough to have a number of exceptional teachers. Tagging along (or, as they liked to think, parent-helping) on field trips and extended projects, I was alerted over and over again to the many ways that creative teachers can venture beyond curriculum requirements to the great benefit of children. As the pressure mounts for school systems to demonstrate performance results in hard, quantifiable numbers, I can't help but hear echoes all the time, echoes that appear in these pages, of Albert Einstein's cautionary injunction, "Not everything that counts can be counted."